Cash In on Laughter

Cash In
on Laughter

INSPIRATIONAL STORIES,
QUOTES, AND QUIPS
ABOUT MONEY AND LIFE

Mary Hollingsworth
GENERAL EDITOR

Guideposts Books
CARMEL, NEW YORK

Editorial, research, and content development managed by Shady Oaks Studio, Bedford, Texas. Team members: Patty Crowley, Vicki Graham, Rhonda Hogan, Mary Hollingsworth, Laura Kendall, Mary Kay Knox, Kathryn Murray, Nancy Norris, Stephany Stevens, Stephanie Terry, and Barbara Tork.

Produced in association with Mark Sweeney & Associates, Bonita Springs, Florida.

www.guideposts.org
(800) 431-2344
Guideposts Books & Inspirational Media Division
Designed by Cindy LaBreacht
Cover by Lookout Design Group
Typeset by Inside Out Design & Typesetting

Printed in the United States of America

Contents

Introduction

Money. In and of itself, it's worthless—just a stack of printed paper, like Monopoly money. What makes our money valuable is what backs it up and what we can trade it for, right? It's backed up by pure gold so we can trade it for all kinds of things we need to make our lives run smoothly, like food and clothing and shelter (minor details).

So why are we publishing a book that focuses on funny things that happen about money? Two reasons: First, God says we shouldn't be so serious and in love with our money, because our money can make us not love other, more important things in life as much as we should. Second, we tend to get really silly about our money—so silly that we do all kinds of crazy things to get it, hang on to it, and spend it. And those silly things we do are often hilarious.

Perhaps then, just perhaps, we might also see some funny things about ourselves when we look in the mirror of our personal finances. After all, a mirror is backed by silver, and we can use it to reflect on our financial attitudes and aptitudes. Mirror, Mirror on the wall, who's really richest after all?

Let There Be Laughter! is a series of books created with one purpose in mind—to brighten your spirit, lighten your load, and give you delightful moments of restorative laughter. We at Guideposts assembled a team to look high and low for funny and wholesome writings that celebrate the lighter side of living. This series is the result of their research. And we hope you have as much fun reading it as they did putting it together.

You'll find stories relating hilarious, real-life tales; rib-tickling jokes and cartoons; absurd, frozen-moment-in-time anecdotes; top-ten lists and other miscellaneous grin-getters; great quotations that make you smile; and some of the best one-liners we've ever seen.

God gave us laughter! And believe it, He knew what He was doing. Because we wish you a dose of healthy fun and inspiration, we give you this book. In the midst of your day-to-day life, may it bring a smile to your face and true joy to your heart.

Let there be laughter!

The Editors

JUST ABOUT THE TIME YOU MAKE BOTH ENDS MEET,
SOMEBODY MOVES THE ENDS.

HERBERT HOOVER

1

Funny Money

What's so funny about money? What's funny is how we act around money. We're just plain silly when it comes to cash. In fact, our money seems to take on a life of its own.

HEY, BROTHER, CAN YOU SPARE A 401(K)?

Many middle-aged people have planned well for retirement. Their savings accounts have grown, their stock investments have paid off, and their retirement plans are all set to kick in. They're prepared.

This chapter is for the rest of us. We who have $2.48 in our savings account, didn't invest in Microsoft because we thought it was a hand cream, and will probably get to our senior years, reach for our nest egg, and realize we already fried it years ago.

I've never been much of a financial wizard. The only portfolio I have is the one I bought at OfficeMax. I have, however, watched everyone around me get rich off their stock market or other investments, while I'm busy looking for a grocery store that has a coin machine where I can cash in my quarters.

Not that my husband and I haven't tried our hand at investing. We have. We just haven't been very successful at it. Take, for instance, the piece of desert property we bought over twenty-five years ago as a retirement investment. It's five and a half acres, and we were told it would eventually be worth well over $100,000.

Today it's not worth much of anything because it has been turned into a sanctuary for an endangered insect. I believe it's in the gnat family. So much for making our fortune there. We've listed it for sale a couple of times, but not many people want to own a government-protected five-and-a-half-acre gnat grazing ground.

Whatever porcelain collectibles I've managed to accumulate over the years haven't paid off either. They actually were increasing in value, but the last Northridge, California, earthquake turned them into mosaic pieces.

> **How about a game show called *Wheel of Missed Fortunes?***

How about a game show called *Wheel of Missed Fortunes?* Contestants could spin the wheel for a dollar amount—$10,000, $50,000, $100,000, and so on. A lovely blonde could stand by the answer board while contestants guessed the cost of their missed investment opportunities or bad business decisions. It might be a depressing show for the contestants, but the viewing audience would feel a lot better about their own bad investments.

It's hard to predict which "sure deal" really will be a sure deal. We don't know if a piece of real estate will cost us a fortune or make us one. The stock market carries no guarantees, either. Gold might be devalued; the company handling our retirement account could default; we could be hit with a catastrophic illness that depletes every dime of our savings. There are no fail-safe ways to wealth, no assurances that the money we save is going to be there for us when we need it. That's why the most important investments we can make aren't financial. They are the ones we make in the lives around us.

Martha Bolton

••

An Advantage of Poverty: Your relatives gain nothing by your death.

Hebrew Proverb

There was once a congregation that was continually asked for money, so often, in fact, that they asked the pastor to speak of them not as his flock but as his fleeced.

James E. Myers

••

REVEREND FUN WWW.REVERENDFUN.COM

©COPYRIGHT GOSPEL COMMUNICATIONS INTERNATIONAL, INC

NO SON, THIS IS YOUR ALLOWANCE, NOT YOUR "DAILY BREAD"

• •

Some philosophers say that money can't talk, but I've got news for them—mine speaks quite clearly. It says, "Good-bye. So long. Farewell. Adieu!"

Mary Hollingsworth

It is difficult to save money when your neighbors keep buying things you can't afford.

Jim Kraus

• •

QUANDARY

If a man runs after money, he's money-mad; if he keeps it, he's a capitalist; if he spends it, he is a playboy; if he doesn't get it, he's a ne'er-do-well; if he doesn't try to get it, he lacks ambition; if he gets it without working for it, he's a parasite; and if he accumulates it after a lifetime of hard work, people call him a fool who never got anything out of life.

Cleon Lyles

PEONIES FROM HEAVEN

Our little stone church predated the Civil War. Now with our congregation bursting with children, we wanted to add a family life center. We had plenty of willing volunteers for raising money and the roof, but as pastor I worried that the work would be too much of a drain on my flock.

Some of the church members went to buy lumber at the mill.

"How much?" I asked them when they got back. "A thousand dollars. We'll need quite a fundraiser to pay for this," one man said.

The men were unloading the lumber when an 18-wheeler turned into our lot. "Someone double-booked this order of plants and flowers," the trucker explained. "My boss told me to donate it to a church or just dump it. You guys interested?"

"Of course," I said. In the back of the truck, an array of peonies, geraniums, and ferns were ours for the taking!

Our plant sale netted $900. Almost the cost of the lumber. And the name of the company that made the mistake. Angel Nurseries.

Steve Wagoner

. . . .

"May I have some stationery?" a man asked the hotel clerk.

"Are you a guest of the hotel?" asked the clerk.

"No, I'm paying eighty dollars a day," said the man.

Tal D. Bonham

. . . .

HAPPY ANYWAY

When I was a little girl, before I started to school, my dad worked for American National Insurance Company in Greenville, Texas—a small, typical East Texas town. His job was to sell life insurance policies and to collect the premiums. And he was good at it. He had a large client route, especially in the lower-income areas of town.

Every week Dad walked through the neighborhoods where his clients lived, knocked on their rickety doors, and picked up their small weekly insurance premiums. The raggedy children in those neighborhoods knew "Mr. Clyde" well and looked forward to his visit. He laughed and teased with them. And they knew he carried a large supply of gum sticks in his pocket to give to his little friends as he went along.

On a few occasions, Dad let me go with him on his route. On one of those days, we walked up onto a sagging wooden porch, and Dad knocked on the door with his usual firm rap. A pretty lady in a clean-but-shabby dress came to the door. When she saw it was my dad, she grinned and said, "Come on in, Mr. Clyde. We're just having a little lunch." So, we went into the front room of the two-room, unpainted, shotgun house.

That's when my preschool eyes went wide at what I saw. Sitting in the middle of the floor were three young children, even younger than I was at the time. And they were, indeed, eating their lunch. Their mother had poured a bowl of pinto beans on the clean-scrubbed floor, and the kids were happily eating them with their hands.

The lady must have seen my shocked expression, and without embarrassment she bent down and looked me right in the eye. Gently she explained, "Sometimes, honey, when you don't have money to buy things, you have to be really creative. Since we can't buy any dishes, my kids and I like to have indoor picnics." And she smiled that happy smile of hers again. Then she calmly returned to her conversation with my dad, who had registered no shock or disapproval. I'm sure he had seen similar situations many times.

I've thought of that experience often through my life, and I have admired that great lady's amazing creativity! She took what she had been given and created something beautiful with it for her children. Using her seeming negatives, she created positive results. She lived in the image of her

> She took what she had been given and created something beautiful with it for her children.

Father and taught me a lesson about money I'll never forget: you don't have to have it to be happy.

Mary Hollingsworth

••

Americans are getting stronger. Twenty years ago it took two people to carry ten dollars' worth of groceries. Today a five-year-old can do it.

Henny Youngman

I have enough money to last me the rest of my life, unless I buy something.

Jackie Mason

••

"Theology has nothing to do with it, Mrs. Westfall. If I bless your lottery ticket, I'll have to bless everybody's."

© Ed Sullivan

Reprinted with permission of the Catholic Exponent, newspaper for the Diocese of Youngstown, Ohio.

A DOLLAR LOAN

A rather frugal man asked the bank for a loan of one dollar and was told he would have to pay seven percent interest at the end of the year. For security he offered $60,000 in U.S. bonds. The banker, foreseeing a potential depositor, accepted the bonds and gave the man a dollar.

At the end of the year, he was back with a dollar and seven cents to clear up his debt and asked for the return of his bonds. Upon returning the bonds the banker asked, "I don't want to be inquisitive, but since you have all those bonds, why did you have to borrow a dollar?"

"Well," said the tightfisted old gent, "I really didn't have to. But do you know of any other way I could get the use of a safety deposit box for seven cents a year?"

Bob Phillips

••

I'm a walking economy. My hairline's in a recession, my waist is a victim of inflation, and together they're putting me in a deep depression.

Joe Taylor Ford

I haven't heard of anybody who wants to stop living on account of the cost.

Abe Martin

••

THE GIVER

*H*e wasn't someone who'd climb the executive ladder, this man I'll call "Ralph." He ran the shipping department of a small company where I worked one year. Built like a bear, his searching eyes almost hidden behind thick-lensed glasses, he put in his hours in a sunless room piled with boxes. Then, his day done, he'd catch a bus home.

I already knew Ralph was a Christian. Somehow he learned I played the violin. Maybe the subject came up in the company's attic lunchroom, as we sat at cast-off tangerine café tables and visited over peanut butter sandwiches and vacuum bottles of soup.

"My daughter wants to learn violin," he said. "There's one we could buy but we don't have enough money for it." When he named the price he could afford, I knew it would buy only a no-frills student violin.

I played a student violin, too. I loved playing violin and studied it through college. Though music didn't become a vocation, I still played in small orchestras, at church, at meetings, even for my grandmother in a nursing home. I knew the positive dimension music brought to my life. I wanted that for Ralph's family.

But Ralph's problem with stretching a paycheck was also mine. Single and thirty years old, I'd just finished two years as a missionary and used up my savings to attend a year of Bible college. Now I was saving for graduate school. What could I do, when I didn't earn much above minimum wage?

When Thanksgiving came, I sensed giddiness among other employees as the finance officer passed out checks. I opened my pay envelope and found my employer's Christmas bonus.

Give it to Ralph, an insistent inner voice said.

But, Lord, I hardly know him, I protested. *You know how much I need to save for college. Every bit helps.*

Give it to Ralph.

God had been working in my heart over the past few years. Living on so little had caused me to pay closer attention to Scriptures that talked about the poor. I had come to understand that God didn't see me as "poor" but rather as one through whom He could bless another.

I was surprised at the joy that replaced my anxiety as I wrote a check equal to the bonus and put it in a card I left on Ralph's workbench. "Please use this toward your daughter's violin," my note said.

A few months later Ralph's family invited me for dinner and a "concert." Three excited children clung to me as I entered their little home with its tired furniture. His wife, her hands knobbed with arthritis, served chicken on mismatched plates. His oldest daughter provided the after-dinner concert on her little violin, playing "Twinkle, Twinkle, Little Star."

I never missed that money. I still had enough for graduate school and for other times God prompted me to give to someone in need. "Cast your bread upon the waters," says Ecclesiastes 11:1. I could only cast crumbs on a vast ocean, but each time I did, I experienced quiet joy in simply obeying God.

Twenty years passed. I married and we had two children. I passed on my love of music by enrolling both children in the school orchestra program. I listened proudly as they learned to play on used violins, advancing from "Twinkle, Twinkle, Little Star" to Bach and Beethoven. My husband's salary as a teacher wasn't extravagant, but it was sufficient for our needs. God allowed me to supplement our income with an at-home business involving a computer. But after ten years that computer was outdated.

The hope of replacing my computer was ended when a drunk driver plowed into our car as we returned home from a weekend away. My husband's last-second swerve to the ditch spared us a head-on collision and possibly our lives, but the

side impact shot glass across our son's face, break-
ing teeth and pocking his face with wounds.
Insurance wouldn't cover all the medical expenses.
The next months were a challenge.

A year later I took my son in for his final plastic surgery to minimize his scars. The appointment
meant not being able to see a Christian friend who
was in town on business. I'd helped him a couple
years earlier with a project that had proven very
successful for him.

The next day, my husband insisted on taking
me out to lunch. Eating out wasn't a high-priority
budget item for us, but he had a two-for-one
coupon.

"You've made some great friends in your work," my husband remarked as we poked chopsticks into our stir-fry. His
remark veiled a secret to which I was not privy. "Let's stop by
a computer store on the way home," my husband said as we
paid for the meal.

"Let's not," I said. "I can't buy one."

I steamed as he pulled me into a local computer store and
started browsing. Still ignoring my pleas to go home, my husband went to find a salesman. Both of them smiled at me.

"A friend of yours was here yesterday," the salesman said,
showing me the friend's business card. And then pointing to
a pile of boxes, he said, "He bought this for you. You're supposed to take it home and enjoy it."

I started shaking and crying as my husband revealed how
this friend had called while I was at the hospital with our son.
My friend said he was obeying a nudge from God by buying
a computer system for me. I couldn't believe that someone
would do this for me. I cried all the way home.

As I started unpacking the computer and figuring out all
its plug-ins, the last part of the verse from Ecclesiastes came

> Insurance wouldn't cover all the medical expenses. The next months were a challenge.

back to me: "Cast your bread upon the waters, for after many days you will find it again."

I had never expected to see that "bread" again, but "after many days" God, the greatest giver of all, had chosen to wash it back ashore in the shape of a computer. I smiled as I thanked Him.

Jeanne Zornes

. . . .

How did a fool and his money get together in the first place?

Kathleen Russell

. . . .

RONALD REAGAN: UNCOMMON CENTS

In Ronald Reagan's first televised budget speech as president, he used a handful of change to illustrate the current value of the dollar.

"It takes an actor to do that," remarked a rival Democrat with grudging admiration. "Carter would have emphasized all the wrong words. Ford would have fumbled and dropped the cash. And Nixon would have pocketed it."

Written from Public Facts

. . . .

Write something that will live forever—sign a house mortgage.

Tal D. Bonham

. . . .

UNDER THE LIGHT

Did you hear about the guy who was down on all fours late one night under a streetlight? He was groping around on the ground, feeling the cement, peering intently at the little cracks.

A friend drove up and asked, "Say, what are you doing there?"

Sam answered, "I lost my wallet."

So the friend got out of his car, walked over, got down on his hands and knees with him, and they both started looking. Neither of them could find it. Finally the friend said to his drunk buddy: "Are you sure you lost the wallet here?"

"Of course not! I dropped it a half a block over there."

"Then why are we looking here?"

"Because there's no *streetlight* over there."

Author Unknown

· ·

Gifts are like bank accounts. They're no good if we allow ourselves to lose interest in them.

Author Unknown

Diamonds are nothing more than chunks of coal that stuck to their jobs.

Malcolm Forbes

· ·

THE LAST NICKEL

A young fellow asked a rich, old businessman how he made his money. The man nodded sagely and said, "It was 1932, the depth of the Great Depression, and I was down to my last nickel.

"I invested that nickel in an apple that I polished all day. At the end of the day, I sold that shiny apple for 10 cents.

"The next morning, I invested those 10 cents in 2 apples. I spent the entire day polishing them and sold them for 20 cents. I continued this for a month and accumulated a fortune of $1.37."

"That's amazing," the young man said.

"Then my wife's father died and left us 2 million dollars."

Jim Kraus

"Dear, your boss just called to tell you
there was a slight mistake in your paycheck."

GIFT GIVING

Sweetie's choices in gifts tend toward the avant-garde (which is French for tasteless and bizarre).

"What's that?" I ask.

"It's Mom's gift," Sweetie says, throwing a box with a picture of a cow on the front into our basket.

"'Genuine Cowpie'," I say, reading the label.

"It's a chocolate pie shaped like . . ."

"I don't think so," I say, handing it back.

"But it's 'udderly delicious,'" Sweetie says.

Last year, Sweetie gave his mother a commode plunger with a Pez dispenser built into the handle.

Then there was the year he dashed into a coin shop five minutes before closing. Nothing says "I love you" like a couple of Susan B. Anthony coins wrapped in a brown paper bag.

If Ripley's Believe It or Not ever opens an outlet mall, Sweetie will be the first in line.

As soon as Mom unwrapped her Gift of the Weird, every eye in the house always rolls my way. I ask you, am I my Sweetie's keeper?

But this year, I am not going to suffer through another humiliating gift opening. I've taken charge of Sweetie's mother's gift, and after eleven months of extensive research, I know exactly what she wants.

There, glittering in the storefront window, like a star in the East, is the perfect gift—a delicate cut-glass crystal nativity scene on a beveled oval mirror.

"She's going to love it," I say, bending over the glass case.

"Austrian leaded crystal," the salesman says, carefully lifting a wise man from the case and holding its twinkling facets to the light.

"I'll take it," I say, whipping out the plastic.

"An heirloom," the salesman says, sticking one of those

mini telescopes in his eye to study the clarity. "Signed by the artist . . ."

"Yeah, yeah," I say. "Wrap her up."

"Perhaps Madam would be interested in the . . . detailing," he says, flipping over the price tag.

After I return from my near-death experience, I regroup.

"I don't suppose you have the same thing in like . . . jelly-jar glass?" I say.

Two cities, three malls, and twenty-nine stores later. . . .

"What's it made of?" I sigh, staring at the dusty display.

Snapping her gum, the salesgirl picks up a Wise Man and bangs him on the countertop.

"Could be glass," she says, listening to the dull clunk.

It is, of course, the last one, and the box is long gone. With the help of a little spit, I scrub off the MADE IN TAIWAN stickers, and drop the little figurines into my basket. Making my way to the checkout, the figurines roll and clink against each other like Coke bottles.

I finally get to the register, and as the checkout girl is dropping Joseph head first into a Certs box, I suddenly panic.

"Wait . . ." I say, picking up the tiny manger, "where's Jesus?"

"Why, he's all around us, dear," the lady behind me says.

"Don't anybody move!" I shout.

Five people throw their arms in the air and someone tosses me their wallet.

Dropping onto all fours, I buff the linoleum as I retrace my path through the store, in search of baby Jesus. I might as well be looking for three wise men and a virgin.

"You'll see," Sweetie says, slapping a used bow on top of the box. "Mom's gonna love it."

Oh yeah, exactly what she's always wanted, The Gift of the Cowpie.

P. S. Wall

••

You know what a YUPPIE is (Young Upcoming Professional), but have you ever heard of DINKs and WOOFs? DINKs = Double Income, No Kids. WOOFs = Well Off Older Folks

Author Unknown

••

FUND-RAISING FOLLIES

If you are a mother with children who are old enough to join an organization or go to school, then you have been baptized in the fires of fund-raising. Whether you help on the committee to dream up great revenue-producing ideas, serve with the hearty souls who administer the fund-raiser, or end up hauling around your offspring door to door, you know firsthand the trials and tribulations of raising money.

We have three children and have lived in many different parts of the country; and I can assure you, fund-raising is not a regional phenomenon. It goes on everywhere. The products may change from place to place (my kids sold *huli-huli* chicken in Hawaii and designer wrapping paper in Virginia), but the techniques and time involved remain constant.

Really smart fund-raisers begin their campaigns by gathering all the children together at a time when their parents are not there, like soccer practice or during lunch at school. They first tell the children the sad tale of how they will be deprived of some wonderful opportunity or piece of equipment because there isn't enough money available. When the kids are convinced of their dire situation, the fund-raising person holds out the only hope in town: the fund-raiser! He regales his potential sales force with tales of abundant resources, rediscovered hope, and, best of all, prizes! Eager hands reach for the sales brochures while visions of compact disc players and bicycles dance in youthful heads.

This is the point at which mothers usually get involved. When those newly inspired salespeople burst in the front door with plans of making the *Fortune* 500 selling greeting cards, mini-pizzas, cinnamon bread, or Christmas wreaths, guess who gets the task of escorting them from customer to customer? My experience tells me that after about a dozen doors, the thrill of door-to-door sales begins to wane. Even if everyone buys something, the salesman's dreams inevitably collide with reality.

"Mom, do you know how many of these I have to sell to earn enough points to get even the Genuine Space Flashlight?!"

"Of course I do. And what's more, the selling is just the beginning. You have to keep records, tally your sales, collect the money, assemble your orders, and then deliver them. "I'm a firm believer in reality.

I actually prefer them because they only cause intense involvement for one or two days and leave you with an empty freezer.

Of course, that's when the little shoulders begin to sag, the bottom lip trembles, the innocent eyes widen, and my resolve starts to erode just the tiniest bit. The next day, Dad takes the brochure to work and leaves it out in a conspicuous place "in case anyone wants to order something." What he's banking on is that everyone walking through the office is also a parent with a kid who is now or has in the past participated in a fund-raiser. It's something you never forget!

By the deadline date most kids haven't sold half of what they anticipated and are in grave danger of losing out on the wonderful opportunity or piece of equipment the funds were intended to purchase. They are convinced they will be the only soccer team without shorts, the only fourth grade that doesn't go to science camp, the only school lacking CD-ROM drives on their computers.

This is when that extra freezer you picked up at the garage sale comes in handy. We have had as many as sixteen loaves of Auntie Belinda's Cinnamon Bread and a dozen of Auturo's Peerless Pepperoni Pizzas in our freezer at one time. And one Christmas many of our dear friends received stationery supplies, wrapped in designer paper—all leftovers from the school sale.

Recently, I've noticed a decline in the popularity of fundraisers which require the kids to sell products door to door. I applaud this trend; however, it hasn't stopped the moneymaking efforts of most schools and organizations, just redirected them. We now have the new, improved, one-time extravaganza fund-raiser—usually a carnival, parking-lot sale, or book fair. I actually prefer them because they only cause intense involvement for one or two days and leave you with an empty freezer.

Last year my daughter's school had a carnival, and I was in charge of the sponge toss booth. It was great fun charging the children to toss soaking sponges at their teachers. And most parents, probably recalling their own school days, seemed eager to finance their children's soggy target practice. We made a healthy, if damp, profit.

Book fairs are perhaps a more civilized way to raise funds. I enjoy working at them because I get to sit in the library and watch all the other mothers get dragged around from display to display by their excited little readers. Book fairs have success written all over them, because parents hardly ever say no to a child who wants to buy reading material, even when they realize Junior's new-found interest in literature is taking a bite out of next month's grocery money. Book fairs really rake in the cash.

This year, my daughter's school is taking a new approach. Parents have the option of either participating in a fundraiser or sending in a check as a donation. Some may find this offensive, but I think it shows a good grasp of economic reality. In fact, I was just getting out my checkbook when the doorbell rang. There on my front porch stood a diminutive entrepreneur dressed in a Sunbeam Girl outfit.

"Would you like to buy a can of caramel corn so my troop can go to camp?" she asked.

I looked down the walkway and spied a mother half-concealed by the hedge.

I sighed and smiled at the little Sunbeam Girl on the porch. "Sure, honey, I'll take two." She brightened, turned, and waved two fingers at her mother, who responded with a "thumbs up" from behind the hedge. Oh well, I already had my checkbook out; and besides, I think her bottom lip was starting to tremble.

Pamela Kennedy

....

Hard work is the yeast that raises the dough.

Anonymous

....

**The Lord loveth a cheerful giver,
but will accept from a grouch.**

BLESSING TREE

I sat in church the Sunday before Thanksgiving, fretting about finances. My husband, Buddy, and I worked hard, but money was short. I'm fixated on my problems. *Lord*, I prayed. *Help me to be thankful.* Then a strange answer came to mind. Popcorn!

At each place setting on our Thanksgiving table I included a dish of unpopped kernels. The "centerpiece" was a big, empty bowl. Then we went around the table. I asked Buddy and the kids to think of things we were thankful for. "Our dog, Cody!" our daughter said.

"Bedtime stories Dad reads us!" one of our sons said. With each blessing, a kernel was dropped into the bowl.

That weekend, we got our Christmas tree, and popped and strung our "blessing popcorn."

Kathy Eblen

MORE THAN COINCIDENCE

I surveyed my new kitchen. The remodeling was finally finished, but not the decorating. Thirty-five feet of countertop sat there almost empty. I'd easily filled nine feet in the old kitchen with a set of pink canisters that matched the curtains I'd put up. Now I dreamed of a blue-and-white theme. But we were out of money. It would have to wait.

Whenever someone came over to visit, we'd sit at the table with a cup of tea and chat. "When are you going to decorate this place?" they asked almost every time.

"One of these days, maybe," I'd say. "I have a blue-and-white theme in mind, but haven't found the right thing just yet." To myself I'd say, *if only I could afford it*.

One day I went into my big walk-in closet, where I like to

pray, and knelt. "God, I'm sorry to bother you," I said. "I don't even know if you care about something this small, but I need help finishing my kitchen. I need something that's just right for me."

Come May, I felt especially embarrassed. I had a full house—my mom and stepdad, seven siblings and their families, grandparents, and assorted aunts and uncles—to celebrate Mother's Day and my birthday, which was a few days later. The counters were still empty.

I'd just opened the card from my sisters, which had a little money in it, when the phone rang. It was a friend. "I'm at a garage sale and I found the perfect blue-and-white dishes for you for next to nothing." I couldn't leave the party, so she asked the woman who was selling them to hold them.

Monday evening, armed with my birthday money, I went to see the dishes. They were perfect in every way—color, size, everything. If I'd had any doubts, they vanished when I flipped over one of the platters and looked at the back.

"The kitchen looks great," a neighbor said the next day. "I love the plates!"

"They were meant for me."

"Why do you say that?" she asked.

I flipped the platter over and showed her. Glazed there was a name, my name: Barbara Wilson.

Barbara Wilson

• •

A guy dies and leaves the shortest will ever. It says, "Being of sound mind, I spent my money!"

Henny Youngman

• •

2

The Other Side of the Coin

*We often flip a coin to determine things. Who
goes first. Who walks the dog. Who gets the
car. But sometimes, it turns out to be "Heads,
I win; tails, you lose!"*

SPEND THE FAMILY FORTUNE NOW

A familiar joke goes like this:

Q. How do you eat an elephant?
A. One bite at a time.

If you've ever been executor of an estate, you have a pretty
good idea of what an elephant tastes like. You know all too
well that the exciting news of receiving an inheritance can be
tempered by the arduous task of liquidating a lifetime of
someone else's assets—one bite at a time. You suddenly find
yourself praying that your newly acquired assets don't
amount to a collection of Chia Pets.

My friend Van experienced this when his elderly parents

died, leaving, for all he knew, almost nothing of value. Although he now had all the keys to the family fortune, he wasn't feeling all that fortunate.

Van grew up in a modest bungalow in Newport News, Virginia, in the fifties. The family's budget was tighter than Joan River's facelift, and pennies were pinched more than a baby's cheeks. Laughter and easy communication were in even shorter supply.

With so few discretionary dollars, Van's mother took up knitting and crocheting. She and her husband also had a pack-rat mentality, which resulted in stuffing the tiny house from top to bottom with "valuables" such as a rhinestone-studded cat clock hung in the kitchen whose tail and eyes darted back and forth with the second hand. Van said that, as a child, the lonely sound of the ticking tail drove him nuts at breakfast every morning.

> Yep, Van's ship had come in all right— packed with enough junk to sink it.

With so much memorabilia, Van began chewing on his white elephant, one bite at a time. For starters, he waded through an extensive collection of dolls with bouffant hairdos and knitted skirts in shades of Pepto-Bismol pink. Then there was a zoo of homemade stuffed animals and complete sets of collector's plates from ritzy restaurants like Kentucky Fried Chicken. Yep, Van's ship had come in all right—packed with enough junk to sink it.

"Katy," he grumbled to his wife, "I'm ready to rent a bulldozer and be done with this! My head is killing me—I need some aspirin." He headed to his parents' tiny bathroom and reached inside the medicine cabinet. As he shook the bottle, comforting white tablets rolled onto his palm, along with a dime.

"Great," he quipped, "I've inherited enough money to buy a gumball." But the bottle didn't feel exactly empty, and he poked his finger into the bottle and pulled out five one-hundred-dollar bills. His headache vanished.

Over the next months, Van found more hidden cash, a valuable coin collection stashed inside the garage wall, an eight-pound silver bar substituting as a doorstop, and his mother's jewelry collection, apparently her one indulgence after the children were grown. He found it lying on the floor in a pile of clothes in a closet. Once he looked over the financial statements, he saw that, though his parents had *lived* frugally, they had *saved* royally.

Van's white elephant estate was turning into a golden goose. Even so, Van would have traded his bird in hand for a childhood filled with family vacations, trips to baseball games with his dad, and a house filled with warmth and laughter.

What kind of inheritance will we leave our children? Are we so focused on living frugally or living comfortably that our priorities are out of whack where the kids are concerned? If so, it's never too late to redefine your priorities and set new goals. Leave your children a *relational* golden goose. Make your home an inviting place to hang out in an atmosphere of warmth and love.

Rachel St. John Gilbert

• •

Rich old people are generally more attractive than poor old people, so by all means, try to get rich before age sets in. Otherwise, you'll just be playing catch-up for the rest of your life and that will just wear you out, let me tell you.

Jill Conner Browne

• •

Ten Ways to Know You've Got a Good CPA

His office is not on the corner of "Walk" and "Don't Walk."

He doesn't take his whoopee cushion to your IRS audit.

He doesn't have to take his shoes off to count to twenty.

His best financial advice is not to stuff your money under your mattress.

His favorite stock is not the Edsel Comeback Corporation.

His calculator doesn't double as a TV remote control.

He doesn't use jelly beans to tally up your tax liability.

He refuses all calls from Enron Rerun Investment, Inc.

His degree is not from Quicken U.

His idea of future security is not to make a list of your relatives who might leave you something in their wills.

Mary Hollingsworth

TOO LATE

The lesson topic was earthly possessions and how individuals put too much value on them. The minister was listing some of these possessions, such as money, fancy homes, recreational toys, and even living possessions such as pets.

He said, "Yes, even our pets can sometimes have more value than they should. But what am I talking about, when I sleep with a dog!" Suddenly there was a heavy silence. He thought to himself, *I wonder if anyone thinks I was referring to my wife.* He cautiously looked across the room and there were a couple of people holding in some pretty explosive laughs. He quickly said, "No, no, I don't mean my wife, I mean JoJo, our dog!"

Too late.

Ken Alley

••

Money can't buy you love, but it sure can make being lonely more comfortable.

Mary Hollingsworth

••

"I was really excited when they told me I'd make $400 a week. Then I found out that meant $7 an hour!"

BUDGET

- A budget is a system of reminding yourself that you can't afford the kind of living you've grown accustomed to.

- A budget is a formula for determining that you need a raise.

- A budget is a sort of conscience which doesn't keep you from spending, but makes you feel guilty about it.

- The bureaucrats in Washington have finally figured out how to balance the budget—they're going to tilt the country.

- Budgeting: A method of worrying before you spend instead of afterward.

Author Unknown

* *

Saddest hour of a man's life is when he tries to get money without earning it.

Horace Greeley

* *

COLLATERAL

A young woman walked into a bank in New York City and asked for the loan officer. She said that she was going to Europe on business for two weeks and needed to borrow five thousand dollars. The bank officer said that the bank needed some kind of security for such a loan, so the woman handed him the keys to a new Rolls Royce parked on the street in front of the bank. Everything checked out, and the bank agreed to accept the car as collateral for the loan. An employee drove the Rolls into the bank's garage and parked it.

Two weeks later, the woman returned, paid the five thousand dollars and the interest, which came to $15.41. The loan officer said, "Ma'am we are happy to have had your business, and this transaction has worked out very nicely. But we are a little puzzled. While you were away, we conducted a more thorough background check and found that you are a multimillionaire. We were wondering why you would bother to borrow five thousand dollars."

The woman replied, "Where else in New York can I park my car for two weeks for fifteen bucks?"

Pam Vredevelt

• •

In a church bulletin these words appeared: "The Lord loveth a cheerful giver. He also accepteth from a grouch."

Lloyd Cory

• •

BALANCED MIND?

Jack Lemmon once found Rita Hayworth working her way through a large pile of letters by tearing them up unopened!

"Stop!" he cried, mortified. "There may be checks in there."

"Oh there are," Hayworth nonchalantly replied. "But there are also bills. I find it evens up."

Clifton Fadiman

∙∙

When a fellow says, "It ain't the money but the principle of the thing," trust me, it's the money.

Elbert Hubbard

Alexander Hamilton originated the put-and-take system in our national treasury: the taxpayers put it in, and the politicians take it out.

Will Rogers

∙∙

SQUEEZING IT DRY

A restaurant owner was convinced that his bouncer was the strongest man around. Hand the bouncer a lemon and he would squeeze it dry. "I'll give $1,000 to anyone who can squeeze out one more drop of juice," the owner announced.

There were numerous attempts, but nobody could do it. One day, a scrawny little man came in and asked to try.

The bouncer grabbed a lemon and crushed it with his bare hand before handing the rind to his competitor.

The scrawny man clenched his fist around the lemon and 20 drops fell into the glass!

"How'd you do that?" the owner asked the winner, counting out the money.

"I work for the IRS."

Jim Kraus

• •

John: Lend me fifty.

Jack: I have only forty.

John: Well, then let me have the forty and you can owe me the ten.

Bob Phillips

My wife found a new way to save her money—she uses mine.

Tal D. Bonham

• •

ADVENTURES IN REALTYLAND

When my husband retired after twenty-eight years in the U.S. Navy, we were ready to settle down. For almost three decades we had moved from coast to coast, living in towns we had never chosen, in houses we never owned. The number one item on our family agenda was to purchase a home. I couldn't wait to have a place where I didn't need to get permission to change the paint or hang wallpaper, cut down a tree or plant a shrub. As soon as we knew where we wanted to live, we started our Adventures in Realtyland.

The first thing we learned is that you need a guide. The guide, commonly referred to as a Realtor, negotiates the jungles of Realtyland, conferring with the natives and translating their unique dialect. This is very important because out in the wilds of the housing market they speak a foreign tongue.

After securing the services of our trusty guide, Valerie, we obtained a copy of the sacred writings titled Multiple Listing Service and headed off to bag ourselves a house. Our assumption that the sacred writings provided clear direction was soon dispelled. When the MLS declared, "creative floor plan with panoramic vistas," we discovered what I would describe as a tree house located at the end of a driveway so steep our wheels spun on the dry pavement. "Handyman's haven" meant there were structural problems serious enough to engage several contractors for months. "Ocean view" actually turned out to be a pie-shaped wedge of blue partly visible from the upstairs bathroom window on a clear day. "Breezy living areas" creatively described a house lacking several windows and a large portion of the roof. Adjectives like *nice, cute, darling,* and *snug* all translate as *tiny* in Realtyland. Phrases such as *great opportunity, needs TLC,* and *priced under market value* are dead giveaways that the place is a dump. When a real estate ad asks you to "use your imagination" as you view a property, you can be sure even Houdini couldn't conjure a way to salvage it. If the décor is described as *cheerful,* you can be certain to find wallpaper with Barney or Big Bird and *well loved* almost always means worn out.

Eventually we were able to decipher a bit of the language in this strange place and even converse with some of the less hostile natives. And with Valerie's diligence and skill we finally found a house that met our needs. This did not mean, however, that our work was finished. Now came the even more daunting task of making the deal.

Now came the even more daunting task of making the deal.

Purchasing in Realtyland is not like going to the store. This is because the prices on houses bear little relationship to what one actually pays. It's sort of like international politics where ambassadors from two hostile nations negotiate a peace agreement that leaves both countries feeling equally frustrated. In the end each country has a vague feeling of loss and nagging doubts about having received the worst end of the deal.

At this point in our adventure, we were required to participate in a mysterious ritual called Escrow. This ritual takes place at a Realtyland shrine: The Escrow Company. Foreigners can't actually watch, but as far as I can ascertain, what happens is this: Money goes into Escrow and special priests and priestesses are paid to pronounce mystical incantations over it. After these ceremonies, the money is distributed to various citizens of Realtyland. I suspect the High Priest, or Escrow Agent, is in cahoots with the rulers of Realtyland because you can't get a house there unless you pay him to bless your money.

If your Real Estate Agent is courageous enough to face down the Angry Sellers and Bluffing Agents inhabiting the jungles of Realtyland and wise enough to placate the High Priests of Escrow, you may end up as we did, the proud owners of a new home. You will have survived one of the most dangerous and intimidating adventures of the twentieth century. But the adventure is not quite over.

It is important to know that those who successfully return from Realtyland often suffer frequent flashbacks. These are characterized by feelings of panic usually occurring at the beginning of the month when the mortgage payment is due. Often there is also a heightened auditory phenomenon causing one to hear termites and carpenter ants gnawing on the support beams under the house. In addition, a sinking sensation has been known to disturb recent homebuyers when the Federal Reserve announces a drop in interest rates. But I have it on good authority that these symptoms gradually disappear and that the best way to hasten their departure is to hang a sign on your front door declaring: HOME SWEET HOME.

Pam Kennedy

• •

In general, the art of government consists in taking as much money as possible from one class of the citizens to give it to the other.

Voltaire

• •

ACME LOAN CO.

"They turned me down — another near-debt experience."

IT'S IN THE BOOK

One Saturday my husband said, "I've written our tithe check. Where should it be put so we'll not forget to take it tomorrow?"

"Stick it in your Bible," I answered. "That's the sure way of getting it there."

We'd barely gotten inside the edifice door the next day when a friend rushed up, eyes lighted, face glowing. "You must see the new pictures of my grandchildren. Got them right here in my Bible."

I admired the kids' photos and was returning them to proud Grandma when I spotted Mary on the far side of the room and threaded my way across the foyer to snag her before she disappeared. "Mary," I said, "Here's a photocopy of that clipping you asked for. I stuck it in my Bible right away so I'd remember to give it to you."

Mary was tucking it between the leaves of her own Bible when a small, hand-written note fluttered to the floor. "Oops," she said, scooping it up. "This is a recipe for hot-fudge topping I promised Betty. She and Bob are hosting an old-fashioned ice cream social for the high-schoolers next weekend."

At that very moment, Betty herself breezed by, grabbed the slip Mary waved at her—like runners passing the torch—tossed a "Thanks!" over her shoulder, tucking it into her Bible for safekeeping.

Inside the ladies' room, two women were discussing an upcoming wedding. "I brought the dress pattern for your bridesmaids' dresses," one said, pulling a fat packet from a guess-what-black-book beneath her arm.

I rejoined Lawrence at the sanctuary entrance, where an usher handed us bulletins which we both promptly stuck in our Bibles. Just then the leader instructed, "Make sure you put today's bulletin into your Bibles; it'll be a handy reference for upcoming events."

Following the service, Lawrence and I trooped upstairs to Sunday school where the teacher told us members, "We'll be using these hand-outs for several sessions so keep them inside your Bibles."

It was near noon when we exited the church and a friend of Lawrence stopped him. "Awhile back you asked for a car mechanic I could recommend. Here's the man's business card. I stuck it in my Bible so I'd not forget to give it to you."

My husband thanked him and inserted the card between the leaves of his own Bible.

So what's my reason for writing this? Well, the next time you hear someone claiming, "It's in the Bible," you'd just better believe it . . . it's probably true.

Isabel Wolseley Torrey

· ·

It's true that two can live as cheaply as one . . . but only half as long!

Author Unknown

· ·

A GOOD TEAM

I looked down at the $10 bill my husband had handed me as I was finishing up the breakfast dishes. "This will barely cover the new textbook I have to get," I protested.

"What more do you want? I'm working two jobs already," Charlie snapped.

"And all I'm doing is the housework, the cooking, and trying to finish my degree. Piece of cake." I grabbed my notebook and stalked out into the rain without another word.

Money, I thought as I drove to the post office to mail my student loan forms. *It's always money.* Charlie and I used to be so good together, but ever since I'd gone back to school, it felt like all we did was argue about how we were going to make ends meet. When we weren't arguing it was only because we weren't speaking.

I ran into the post office. By the time I got the forms mailed class was about to start.

"Miss? Excuse me, miss," someone said as I hurried to my car. An elderly woman waved to me. "Could I trouble you for a ride? I need to take these pills to a friend downtown." She pulled a white pharmacy bag out of a pocket of her old coat.

"I'm sorry," I said, "but—"

"Please, I wouldn't ask unless I really had to," she pleaded. "I prayed for God to send me a kind-hearted soul, and when I saw you, I knew you were the one."

Yeah, right, I thought, recalling how nasty I'd just been to my husband. I'm sure I'm one of God's favorite people today. In fact I hadn't felt much of God in my life at all lately. But I couldn't leave this poor lady stranded in the rain. "Okay," I said, "but we have to get a move on."

My companion introduced herself as Mary and, in between giving directions while I drove, rambled on about herself and her husband. Apparently they had fallen on hard times. "How about you, dear?" she asked. "Are you married?"

"Yes," I said, not really listening.

"That's wonderful. It's so good to have a partner," she said. "My husband and I don't have much, but we have each other—and of course, our faith in God. Even now when our heat and hot water are out and we don't have enough for a decent meal, we don't lose heart. We know he watches over us. Look how he sent you to help me today! Oh, right over here, dear." I pulled into her friend's apartment complex.

> "My husband and I don't have much, but we have each other— and of course, our faith in God."

Suddenly I thought of the $10 bill in my purse. *I could borrow the textbook from the library and give her the money instead*, I thought. But all I said was, "Good luck, Mary."

"Thank you, dear," she said, getting out of the car. "God bless you."

All day I kept thinking about Mary. She'd looked worn out. Yet she had found a way to help a sick friend.

She was still on my mind that evening. Sitting at dinner with Charlie, I imagined Mary and her husband in their unheated apartment. We were having a tough time getting by, but at least we were warm. At least we could put food on the table.

While we were doing the dishes I found myself telling Charlie about Mary. "I know we need that money, but I feel awful," I said. "What if that were us?" All of the frustration and uncertainty of the past months caught up with me. I'm so turned around about money I turned my back on someone in need. I started to cry.

Charlie pulled me into his arms. "So what do you want to do?" he asked.

"I'd like to take her some groceries. But I don't even know her last name or where she lives," I said.

"You know where her friend lives, right? It's a start. We'd better hurry before the store closes."

At the grocery store we zipped down the aisles together, picking up basics. Then Charlie threw in a box of candy; I grabbed some nice soap. When I saw the total on the cash register, I sucked in my breath. Charlie squeezed my hand. "Don't worry," he said. "We'll still be all right."

Charlie drove while I tried to remember the way to Mary's friend's place. *It feels so good to be working together for a change,* I thought as we arrived at the apartment complex.

Inside the lobby was a giant panel with rows of buzzers. Mary had said her friend lived alone so I started to search for single women's names. My heart sank when I saw that there were no names on the buzzers—just apartment numbers.

"I'm sorry, honey," Charlie said. "At least we gave it a try."

"I know, I know," I sighed, slumping against the wall. Lord, why isn't anything working out . . .

A crackling came from the bank of buzzers. "Hello? Who's there?" a woman's voice asked.

I had accidentally pressed a buzzer when I leaned against the wall. I looked at Charlie.

"Give it a shot," he whispered.

"I'm sorry to bother you," I said. "I'm looking for a lady I gave a ride to today. She was bringing medicine to a friend."

"Oh, you must mean my friend Mary," the woman said. "She was here earlier with my pills."

In no time we were at Mary's apartment. "Hi, Mary," I said. "I hope we're not disturbing you, but . . ."

. . . We brought you a few things we hope you can use,"
Charlie continued, carrying in the shopping bags.

"God bless you!" Mary exclaimed. "I'm going to be
praying for you two."

We were quiet on the way home. Not the kind of silence
that had been coldly punctuating our recent disagreements,
but a peaceful, content silence, the kind that can help hold a
marriage together.

We were a pretty good team, Charlie and me. We always
had been. It just took Mary to remind us.

Donna M. Collins

. . . .

**In every insurance policy the big print giveth and
the small print taketh away.**

Author Unknown

. . . .

INFLATION AND THE TOOTH FAIRY

Our oldest son, Jerome, and his friend Josh were insepa-
rable. Born just days apart, they became fast friends the
day we moved into the neighborhood, when they were four.
They did everything together; building forts, riding bikes,
playing ball, and even losing their first tooth just days apart.

Josh was the first to lose his bottom, front tooth, and since
"Josh said it didn't even hurt," we were able to talk Jerome
into letting us pull the now hanging tooth. There had been
much crying and fretting, but at last Jerome held his tiny
tooth in his hand. Oh, what joy for us to finally have the
"deed" done! "I'm going to go get my tooth fairy pillow!" he
exclaimed happily.

While in preschool he had received a small heart-shaped pillow with a little pocket on the outside to hold a lost tooth. He carefully wrapped the tooth in tissue and placed it in the pocket before saying, "Now I'm going to get my twenty bucks from the Tooth Fairy!"

My husband and I stood there speechless. I am sure the color must have drained from my face as Jerome went on to explain that Josh had gotten a twenty-dollar bill under his pillow for his tooth.

My color came back quickly as I became slightly irritated. My first thought was, *Who in the world gives their kid twenty dollars for a lost tooth?* However, it didn't take me long to realize there must be some sort of explanation, since I knew Josh's parents to be good, common-sense people. I quickly came up with a potential "out" for our less wealthy tooth fairy. "Well . . . I think the Tooth Fairy made a mistake. I think she probably couldn't see very good in the dark and grabbed a twenty-dollar bill by mistake."

"Nope," Jerome replied, "things just cost more nowadays. When you and Dad were little, you used to get only a *quarter!*"

My husband, who is an accountant, stifled a laugh.

I had to do some fast talking (it's called lying) to convince Jerome that the Tooth Fairy must have made a mistake. I explained to him that I thought the going rate for a first tooth was probably five dollars and a dollar or two for each tooth after that. I then went on to make up a cockamamie story about the amount depending on what kind of shape the tooth was in. This did not convince him a bit because he was *sure* his teeth were in better shape than Josh's. Finally, after his dad backed up my story, Jerome seemed able to accept the idea that he was probably going to receive five dollars.

Because he was so excited that night, it took him a long time to go to sleep. I awoke to the sound of his near hysterical voice, "The Tooth Fairy didn't come! My tooth's still *here!*" My eyes flew open and my heart began to pound as I realized that the "tooth fairy" fell asleep while waiting for Jerome to fall asleep.

I ran over to him to console him saying, "Here, let me help you look. . . ."

Sure enough, I "found" a five dollar bill down in the covers. I exclaimed, "See . . . I *told* you that the Tooth Fairy can make mistakes! She didn't put the money under your pillow . . . she put it in your bed. She probably didn't know that your tooth was in the special pillow! She'll be back tomorrow for it, I'll bet!" (More lies.)

Jereome nodded in agreement and said, "Maybe she got scared off by Dad's snoring!" We both laughed. Then, despite the fact that his tooth had been forgotten, his grin grew wider as he said, "Told you things cost more nowadays!"

Elizabeth Schmeidler

••

When it comes to money, always be sure to act your wage.

Author Unknown

••

3

Shop 'Til You Drop!

Megamalls, strip shopping centers, super-stores, and catalogs. Online and over the phone. In person and from the car. We're crazy about shopping! And shopping offers many opportunities to cash in on laughter.

TAKE OUR MONEY . . . PLEASE

I don't know about you, but I resent it when advertising companies target younger audiences over older ones. We're just as important, aren't we? We like to spend money, don't we? One look at an outlet mall will tell you, we are a shopping force to be reckoned with.

So why aren't more marketing companies targeting our age group? Why are there so many youth-oriented programs and advertisements on television today? Why are we being ignored? Don't companies realize they are missing a huge market?

Now granted, a visit to the local mall will show you there are a lot of teenagers hanging out there these days. But are they shopping? Are they spending money? No. They're "hanging." Contrary to what our skin might be doing, we members of the over-forty crowd don't "hang." We shop, and not just window shop either. We're serious buyers. When we pick up an item and turn it over to see the price, we often carry it right on over to the checkout counter and pay for it. Why? Because we know the energy involved with picking up items. We don't do it unless we're committed.

If you're still not convinced that middle-agers and seniors are the more dedicated shoppers, then ask yourself this question: *When is the last time you saw a seventeen-year-old pushing one of those little wheeled carts full of packages through a department store?*

I rest my case.

Teenagers don't push wheeled carts. They put whatever they buy in their backpacks or pockets. How much can pockets hold?

Barely anything. Even a backpack is limited. But a wheeled cart has plenty of space, and we are the kings and queens of the wheeled cart. Nothing holds a blanket, a box of Epsom salt, and a bag of prunes better than a wheeled cart. Sure, we may have rolled over a few toes in our rush to a Bluelight Special at Kmart, but the public needs to know that when we are on a mission for bargains, we take no prisoners.

We don't only patronize discount stores, shopping malls, and outlet stores either. We buy from catalogs, television shopping networks, and door-to-door salesman who are one sale away from winning a trip to the Bahamas. It doesn't matter that we have never been to the Bahamas ourselves; we'll buy whatever we have to in order to help a total stranger get there.

We're trendsetters, too. Do you really think that teenagers were the ones who started the baggy-

> We're trendsetters, too. Do you really think that teenagers were the ones who started the baggy-pants craze?

pants craze? They weren't. Let me remind you that grandpas have been wearing baggy pants for years. But did clothing manufacturers ever jump on this idea and market the look to Grandpa's age group? Have you ever seen a Calvin Klein commercial with an eighty-year-old shirtless man, wearing pants two sizes too big and hiked up to his armpits, saying "Just be"?

I don't think so. But they took this look and aggressively marketed it to teenagers. Teenagers in their big, baggy pants aren't original. They're not trendsetters. They're just wannabe grandpas.

Another trend that teenagers get credit for starting, but they didn't, is all these wild hair colors. Have they forgotten who it was who started the blue hair trend? Grandmothers. But has one of these lovely ladies ever been offered her own show on MTV? Have they ever been featured on the cover of *Rolling Stone* or *Entertainment Weekly?* Do they get any credit for their hipness?

No, like Grandpa, their style is copied with no credit given.

But by overlooking the middle-age and senior crowd, advertising executives are missing out on a huge market. Our demographic buys a lot more than just shoe inserts, corn pads, age-defying face creams, and support hose. We buy toys and computer games for our grandchildren, nieces, nephews, friends' children, and yes, even for ourselves sometimes. We buy clothes and household goods, computers and compact discs (even though the word disc makes us a little nervous). We buy high-ticket items, low-ticket items, and everything in between. Contrary to what you may think, limited budget doesn't mean broke. We'll spend, but we just want a good value for our money.

We buy furniture, clothes, makeup, purses, shoes, carpets, vacuum cleaners, ride-on lawn mowers, hot-water heaters, cars, and major appliances. You won't find all that on a teenager's shopping list.

We also pay for household repairs, patronize hair salons, restaurants (both fast-food and fine dining), and we go on trips (not just cruises or road trips in our Winnebagos; many of us still take business trips).

So why then aren't the marketing people targeting our demographic more often? Young professionals may make more money than us annually, but they've got $4.98 in their savings account. We may make less than they do, but we have substantially more in our savings accounts to spend. I myself am up to nine dollars now.

I suppose it will take a while to change the thinking of these advertising executives, so we'll have to be patient. In the meantime, we'll just have to continue doing what we've done all along: shop. Spend our money. And keep watching all those Calvin Klein commercials with their "hip" teenagers modeling those baggy britches, knowing all along that Grandpa could be doing a much better job.

Martha Bolton

∙∙∙

I won't say my wife is a big spender, but Macy's just opened a branch in our living room.

Bob Phillips

It is good to have things that money can buy, but it is also good to check up once in a while and be sure we have the things money can't buy.

George Horace Lorimer

∙∙∙

REVEREND FUN WWW.REVERENDFUN.COM

©COPYRIGHT GOSPEL COMMUNICATIONS INTERNATIONAL, INC.

BILL   BILL   BILL   BILL

YEA, THOUGH I WALK THROUGH THE VALLEY OF DEBT

20 Great Things You Can Still Buy for Less Than a Dollar (if You're Careful Where You Shop)

A pack of Clove or Black Jack gum

A dip of double-fudge chocolate ice cream

A Bic ballpoint pen

A cherry vanilla Coke

French fries

A box of paperclips

A newspaper with color comics

A McDonald's cheeseburger

Hershey bar with almonds

A 40-watt light bulb

A pack of No. 2 pencils

A small bag of buttered popcorn

A greeting card and matching envelope

Two first-class postage stamps

Mint-flavored dental floss

A package of flower seeds

A rainbow snow cone

A box of Crayola crayons

A small American flag

Anything in a Dollar Store!

Mary Hollingsworth

20 Important Things Money Can't Buy (No Matter Where You Shop)

A true friend

Peace of mind when facing death

Respect

Joy in spite of pain

Good health

Happy dreams

Faith in troubled times

Home

More time

A baby's dimpled smile

Hope

A gentle spring breeze

Freedom

Happiness

God's grace

A sweet summer rain

Trust

Pure mountain air

The loyalty of a good dog

Love

Mary Hollingsworth

DAD, I NEED A . . . WHAT?

The boy was about to turn ten. That's a big age for a kid because they're now close to being a teenager, which is close to being a high schooler, which is close to being a quasi-adult with pimples.

Yeah, turning ten is a pretty big deal.

He tossed a Nerf football in my direction. I snagged the ball close to the tree where the dog does his business and tiptoed into the driveway. At this point, I didn't realize how out of touch I was with the world of today's ten-year-old boy. That would soon change.

I tossed the football back.

"I've been thinking about what I want for my birthday," the Boy said, pulling the ball out of the air.

I smiled. I remembered when I was a kid. Heck, he probably wants a BB gun, a video game, a puppy, a new baseball mitt . . .

"I need a cell phone," he said, tossing the football in a pretty tight spiral.

The ball hit me in the chest and bounced precariously close to the tree.

"What?"

At his age, all I *needed* for my birthday was a GI Joe with Kung Fu Grip. I didn't need a cell phone.

OK, OK, so the closest thing to cell phone technology I'd seen as a kid was on *Star Trek*. The point is I wanted a toy, not a piece of communication equipment capable of connecting me with people who don't even speak English. The only way I'd have possessed something like that as a kid is if I'd been a spy for the Russians . . . which I wasn't.

"I need a cell phone," he said again, running toward me to pick up the ball and toss it back. This time I caught it.

"You don't need a cell phone," I told him. "Cell phones are the gifts that keep on taking. If I buy you a cell phone, we have to keep giving the cell phone company money month after month after month. Besides, cell phones are for adults, Mulder and Scully, teenage girls and crack dealers. You're not a teenage girl, are you?"

"No," he said. "But I still need a cell phone."

I frowned at the boy. The last thing he really, really wanted was Pokémon bed sheets. Now he *needs* something so he can talk to kids he'll see at school anyway. What will he talk to them about? Probably his really cool Pokémon bed sheets.

I felt the need, as Dad, to use my superior height, weight and upper body strength to put the boy in his place. I threw the Nerf ball like a rocket toward him. He caught it anyway.

"Why do you need a cell phone?" I asked, putting the appropriate stand-up comic emphasis on the word 'need.'

"Because kids my age on TV have cell phones."

That's it. I knew cable television would signal the apocalypse.

> I knew cable television would signal the apocalypse.

"Kids your age on TV are secret agents, billionaires and spaceship pilots—all of whom can buy their own cell phones," I said. "When you're one of those, we'll talk."

I threw the ball at him and he dropped it.

Yeah, the boy's growing up, but Dad's still king.

Jason Offutt

A lot of money is tainted. It taint yours and it taint mine.

Author Unknown

Gambling is a way of getting nothing for something.

Wilson Mizner

Keep your lives free from the love of money and be content with what you have, because God has said, "Never will I leave you; never will I forsake you."

Hebrews 13:5

... And help us to balance our books tonight. Amen.

IT'S ONLY MONEY

I don't understand why "disagreement over finances" consistently rates as one of the key problems married couples face, especially when the Visa people have thoughtfully arranged a system whereby we can keep spending and spending even when we don't have any money. What's to disagree over? It's basically like having unlimited cash. I don't know why my wife can't grasp this self-evident fact.

Credit cards are tremendously convenient. I have a gob of them in my wallet (and even more of them in my dresser drawer), and the U.S. Postal Service brings me a new batch of offers almost daily. In many cases, the credit card companies offer to give me a bunch of free stuff if I just agree to use their cards.

"Hey, look!" I called to Dale one day as I brought in the mail. "We got a credit card application from an airline. We can earn free tickets to anywhere if we just charge some stuff! I think I'll sign us up."

"It's a scam, just like the scam about getting money toward a car," Dale replied. "Read the fine print, and you'll discover that you have to buy $1,000,000.00 worth of stuff at a non-competitive interest rate to get a so-called 'free' flight."

Dale has serious skepticism issues. I try to give the Visa folks the benefit of the doubt, preferring to believe the best about people. I am optimistic in that way. Dale, on the other hand, has been known to shred mail without even opening it, even if the envelope very clearly states, *"You can't afford to miss out on this offer! Respond at once, or you will contract scurvy!"* Like I want to risk contracting the same disease that plagued the crew of the *Santa Maria?*

Dale and I have very different approaches to spending, but I don't allow this to be the source of conflict in our home. On the contrary, the conflict usually happens outside our home when we are on vacation and I decide to make an impulse purchase with a credit card.

We were close to 200 miles from home during one vacation when we happened upon a "specialty item" store that had a small stock of solar-paneled, tan-colored pith helmets at an incredibly reasonable price. I tried one on, and it was awesome. I mean, a regular British-style pith helmet would have been great, but this model had a small fan built right into the top of it. All I needed to do was step into the sunlight, and the solar panel converted the energy into a cooling breeze. It was a truly exceptional find, and I had never seen a helmet like this anywhere else.

"I'm going to get one," I told Dale.

She looked at the price tag. "Fifty dollars?" she gasped. "What in the world are you thinking?"

"Not to worry, my sweet," I replied. "I just happen to have a credit card on me."

"Which makes it free?" she asked, arms folded.

"Basically," I said. "They don't charge us interest for thirty days, so it is like getting a free loan. Besides, if things get a little tight, I can just stretch out the payments."

"You're right!" she exclaimed. "You could just add this charge to the tacky Sumo wrestler doll you bought across the street a few minutes ago, and all the other weird toys you have been buying with reckless abandon. You could just pay the minimum on all your credit cards and stretch out the payments forever!"

"That's the spirit!" I replied. "With any luck, I'll be dead before they are paid off."

"Dave, the credit card companies absolutely love people like you," Dale stated.

I blushed at the compliment. "I suppose that's why they keep sending me all those nice offers."

She made me put the helmet back on the rack and threatened to eliminate ten of my credit cards if I tried to make any more unbudgeted purchases.

> **Dale likes to mull over her spending decisions, sometimes for years.**

Dale likes to mull over her spending decisions, sometimes for years. I mulled once for about five minutes, but I didn't like it, so I stopped. It isn't like I horribly overspend or don't pay my bills. I do pay them. I just don't monitor them as closely as Dale. She thinks we should track all of our bills monthly and know precisely how much we owe. She also thinks it is a good idea to balance the checkbook, which I think is the most boring task imaginable. "We still have checks, so what's the worry?" is my financial motto.

When it comes to fiscal matters, I am waaaaaaay more flexible than Dale. But because I want to be happily married—as opposed to hospitalized—finances are an area in which I have had to do some changing in order to adapt to her comfort level.

For instance, I have learned that my impulse spending can ruin a vacation for her. If there is ever a time when I am tempted to go into spending mode, it's when we are on vacation. But many activities or purchases that I consider fun, she considers wasteful and even stupid. (The people who make wind-up, chattering teeth will *never* make a sale to Dale. I, on the other hand, have purchased several pairs over the years. One never knows when one will need a backup pair, perhaps as an emergency wedding gift.)

Dale can't really relax and have fun on a vacation unless she incorporates at least a measure of frugality into the planning and execution of the trip. So if we are driving to our destination, she will often pack food. My tendency is to simply pull into a burger joint along the way and buy food whenever we are hungry. But I have gotten used to the fact that we are going to have cheese and crackers, salami, apple slices, carrots, trail mix, and that kind of stuff in the car on a long trip. If we do that, then Dale can enjoy eating out periodically without worrying about how much we are spending. And I have come to grips with the fact that we are also going to take some extra time to look for package deals, special prices on accommodations, and discounts on activities.

Frankly, Dale's approach has saved us a *lot* of money over the years, and I have to admit that I have not suffered many ill effects from missing out on all those opportunities to visit fast-food joints off the freeway, even though Dale makes me include roughage in my diet.

But while I have learned to moderate my purchasing habits for Dale's sake, she has likewise moved in my direction. I do *not* like to shop. I do not like to agonize and dither and hesitate over a mere purchase. I like to walk in, find what I like, buy it, and leave in just about as much time as it took you to read this sentence. I consider shopping a necessary evil, an unfortunate requirement, a baneful responsibility. She thinks it is a delightful challenge, a competitive sport, a jolly romp. So we both have had to budge to avoid driving each other crazy.

Sometimes my "strike-while-the-iron-is-hot" viewpoint is a better approach than Dale's "let's-think-this-over-for-a-few-decades" approach. This was nowhere more apparent than when we were trying to purchase a house in the middle of a hot real-estate market in the summer of 2002. Houses were selling within days of being listed—and sometimes within hours. It was pure insanity. There was even one instance where a guy was talking with his wife over breakfast, and he casually asked, "What do you think about putting our house on the market?" Suddenly, four real-estate agents leaped through the window, wrestled him to the floor, and gave him noogies until he agreed to sign a contract.

Dale and I had been looking at houses for weeks, but other buyers were always beating us to the finish line. We had to reorient our lives completely during those weeks so that the split second our agent phoned us, we could drop whatever we were doing and race to another newly listed home before the rest of the mooing stampede of buyers arrived.

One day our agent called about yet another home, and even though the timing was not terribly convenient, I leaped out of the chair and told the dentist he could finish the filling later.

We walked into the house. I looked around the living room for precisely five seconds (I am not exaggerating) and told the agent, "We'll take it."

"Can we at least see all the rooms?" Dale asked.

We wasted five entire minutes poking around the place, and then Dale agreed that we should make an offer. But, alas, we were too late. Someone had already made an offer that was accepted even though our offer would have been higher.

I made a backup offer, but the listing agent told us not to get our hopes up. "The first offer is very solid, so I would advise you to keep looking," she said. "You need to mentally let this one go."

Deflated, Dale and I decided to reconsider the whole idea of buying a home. The market was too intense. We went home and started planning possible modifications to our existing house.

A week later, I was 500 miles away on a business trip when my cell phone chirped. It was the Realtor. "Mr. Meurer, the house you wanted is available," she said. "The other escrow fell through. You are the first person on my list to call, but I have several others. If you want the house, I need to know immediately."

I asked her to give me ten minutes so I could call Dale. I was elated as I punched in our home number, but by the time the phone rang I had a sinking feeling in my chest. Dale and I had pretty much decided against buying a house, and we had mentally shifted gears into the "let's-just-add-a-room" mode. I was used to making quick decisions, but I was pretty sure that Dale would not be willing to make a huge financial commitment under a five-minute deadline. She would probably want to see the house again, talk it over, run the numbers, ask advice—all reasonable desires, but impossible under the circumstances.

She answered the phone.

"Hi, Hon," I said. "The house is for sale again. The agent just called. But she has a bunch of interested parties, so you literally have to decide right now if you want it. I hate to spring this on you, but that's the scoop. What do you want to do?"

I braced for what I knew would be the answer. She didn't want to rush into a decision like this, and we had already come to grips with staying in our current home, especially since we had fixed it up to sell so it was in better shape than ever, we had so much history in it, the yard was perfect for having friends out on the deck, and it was cheaper to just stay where we were . . .

"Let's take it," she said.

"What did you just say?" I asked, blinking.

"Tell her yes," Dale answered.

"Dale, did you just make an instant decision about a financial matter?" I asked.

"I learned it from you," she said.

So we bought the house.

As with so many other areas of life, we have changed each other when it comes to making financial decisions. We have learned from each other's perspectives, benefited from each other's strengths, and adapted to each other's desires.

Because of Dale, I am less rash than I would otherwise be. And because of me, Dale has become less guilt-ridden about spending a few bucks. The combination has worked out pretty well. However, with all the money we saved, you'd think she could cut me some slack on the solar-powered pith helmet.

She did ultimately strike a deal with me. "Dave, in the event you ever take a trip to Egypt without me, you can buy the ugly helmet."

I think I got the bad end of that bargain.

Dave Meurer

· ·

Whenever my wife needs money, she calls me handsome. She says, "Hand some over."

Bob Phillips

If you want to know what God thinks of money, look at the people he gives it to.

Bob Phillips

· ·

"Our terms are net 30 days. If you don't pay after 30 days, we come after you with a net!"

Pray to God for a good harvest, but don't stop hoeing.

Bohemian Proverb

DUMB THINGS I HAVE DONE IN HIGH-END DEPARTMENT STORES

Lest you think I'm above shopping craziness, let me relate a true tale. The stupidest purchase I ever made was when I was limited for time, feeling fat, and had a blind date with a guy whose photo looked so much like Tom Cruise. I spent way too much money on an outfit that slimmed my backside about an inch but didn't look particularly great overall. (I only noticed this a week later.) I wore the outfit so infrequently that the CPW (cost per wearing) was exorbitantly high.

I actually repeated this shopping mistake. (Note to self: Never go shopping for outfit that I absolutely need in twenty-four hours to make me look ten pounds thinner on first date. If must buy something, settle for new lipstick, then head home to soak in bath and figure out clever hairstyle.)

Only twice in my life have I bought an outfit for a specific date. So fitting it was that both dates had to be canceled! One was with an ex-boyfriend, and it's probably a jolly good thing we never reconnected. The second was for the Cruise look-alike, who, after he saw my photograph, apparently decided I wasn't Gwyneth Paltrow enough. Another save!

So I had two beautiful overpriced outfits, one so tight I couldn't breathe while sitting; the other looked sloppy as it grazed my curves. This is what happens when you buy in a panic, or with way too much thought for your hips.

The fact is, shopping for the wrong reasons has enormous downsides. When we focus on our own needs, wants, and desires, we become ingrown and selfish—I believe a part of us actually starts to atrophy or rot. We can no longer see others' needs because we are mesmerized by the things we aspire to acquire. We lose awareness, becoming desensitized to the needs of the hungry, poor, lonely, and homeless—the neighbor who needs bus fare and grocery money. We become conscientious objectors in the war on poverty and do not recognize our resources as the opportunity they present. We cannot comprehend others' needs when we are looking at ourselves. For many of these same reasons, alcoholics turn to their numbing devices. Others raid the fridge. Still others don outfits four sizes too small and head out on the town looking for attention and getting it, but not the kind that makes their hearts swell with true joy.

I long ago discovered that when I am at my most emo-tionally desperate place is when I have the greatest need to reach out and give to others, experiencing empathy with their needs. That heals. Shopping doesn't.

Sharon Durling

....

When it comes to money, Death is a thief you cannot stop—you *will* leave home without it.

Rick Atchley

....

HOW TO SUCCEED IN BUSINESS . . .
REALLY TRYING

Talk about low man on the totem pole! I couldn't even get near the totem pole during those early years of my driving work. Maybe it hurt so much because I wanted to drive so badly. I had started out driving my daddy's farm truck in Hayneville, Alabama. I was only eleven then, but when I got my hands on that wheel and guided that machine down those red clay ruts, I knew that big truck and I were close friends.

But that old truck wasn't going to take care of eight brothers and sisters. So, soon as I was old enough, I headed for Chicago where I went to work in a factory. I worked my way up to a good job, but every time I saw a big diesel rig snorting toward the city limits I'd get the same feeling I'd had as a little boy lying on my cot and hearing the semis double clutch and roar as they bit into the grade on U.S. 31.

Finally I saved enough money to buy a second-hand tractor rig and started hauling, from Chicago to New York, from Cleveland to St. Louis. But I just couldn't make it pay off; the good driving feeling was there but the money wasn't. Besides, there was something else. I guess it really hit me when I'd see them on the road—those cross-country buses hissing by me in the rain.

In 1958 after moving to New York City, I applied for a job as driver with a charter bus company. They took me on as a standby on the night shift. I got a run only when one of the regular men didn't show up.

Finally I got disgusted and left for another charter company; but it was just the same. Sometimes I'd buy a run from a driver, pay him to take his trip and off I'd go under his name. I'd notice the cost details on each trip and talk with the dispatcher and mechanics.

For I had a dream. The only thing was, it involved $25,000. That's what I'd need to buy a good used bus. And here I was, making $13 a day as a standby.

But I remembered something my mother always told me: "It's up to you to take the first step. That shows the good Lord you're serious about what you want to do, and then He will help you."

I enrolled in a diesel mechanic's school in Bergenfield, New Jersey. I paid five dollars a lesson, which lasted from seven p.m. to midnight, three nights a week. I did this three years steady until I'd dream about piston rings and crankshaft tolerances.

During this time, I started saving in a bank near me. Every time I saved a hundred dollars, I'd use it to borrow another hundred and added that to my savings. This way I kind of leapfrogged my account ahead. Finally I had $5000. I had a feeling then as if the Lord said, "O.K., you've taken some steps; now I'm going to show you a bigger one!"

I heard about a GMC diesel, 37-passenger bus for sale at a low figure, low enough to swing it with my savings and a loan. Only one thing was missing: an engine. Now that mechanic's course would come in handy.

My wife Frankie got a job working in a restaurant, and for the next six months I spent every spare hour with my tool kit, engine manual and an old engine that was little more than junk.

Then came the day I fired it up and for a minute I just listened to its music, I got into the driver's seat, and like an uncaged bird my bus and I hummed along the highway to Brooklyn where I already had a name picked out—B&C Bus Lines.

We'd go to other charter bus companies for jobs. Sure, I still got the leftovers, but now I was driving my own business.

Within two years I was able to borrow money on this first bus to buy another. By 1965 I had five buses and was providing jobs for people in my neighborhood.

Then the trouble started.

My overhead was climbing like the temperature in some of my radiators. Also, I had no garage and had to park my buses in vacant lots. Just try to fix an engine in the snow!

On top of it all I was falling behind in my repayments. There was only one earthly thing that could help and that was money.

One cold morning I walked out to the lot where those five buses sat. One had developed a flat in the night and I felt as low as that tire. I swung up into the driver's seat of old number one and sat there, wondering if I should just sell out and go back to being last man on the night shift again.

I leaned against that cold steering wheel. *Oh, Lord*, I thought, *I have faith and will take any step. But right now I don't know which direction to take.*

Snow flicked against the windshield. And then I began to get that feeling, the same one I had when I first saw this bus. Only this time it was: "See the Chase Manhattan Bank." I almost laughed out loud. The Chase Manhattan Bank! Maybe if I was Greyhound or U.S. Steel.

But the feeling got stronger. So I contacted the bank.

I couldn't believe it. The man I talked to seemed interested; he wanted to know more about my business. From then on the bank and I spent a lot of time together. They helped me organize my operations and came through with a loan which not only helped pay off my debts but enabled me to get a garage.

Today, B&C Lines has fifteen buses on the road. And I like to think we're helping make many people happy—whether we're taking families to a church picnic or a high school class to Washington, D.C.

The other day one of my drivers was ill and I took his run. As my wife, now our office manager, waved me out of the garage, I chuckled; after all this time, it looked like I was still on standby.

As the tires sang beneath me, I thought of the miles that had gone by since I first drove dad's old truck down those clay ruts. And then I thought of mother standing in front of her Sunday school class saying: "Children; you take that first step and the Lord will help you the rest of the way."

"You're so right, Mama," I whispered.

Bill Logan

• •

You can't take it with you—did you ever see a hearse pulling a U-Haul?

Author Unknown

• •

MONEY MUSINGS

I look around and see legions of people living the American Dream. We are surrounded by nice cars, spacious homes, manicured streets, and a terrific school system. For all intents and purposes, we have "arrived."

Lately, however, I have worried about how we can maintain this standard of living. After all, I'm kind of attached. What is this thing called "money" and how do we have so much of it?

I believe that money is a figment of our imagination. Once upon a time, it was born to facilitate trade (since buckskins are so heavy to carry), but it has since grown into a comic abstraction. Money refers to a mass of numbers, or concepts, floating through the air. We call this "cash flow." When our trees need trimming, we dip our finger into the cash flow and fling some at the gardener. When our car needs gas, we pull up to the pump and swipe some data through the machine. Some gas stations allow you to wave your data at the machine. With Direct Deposit, we don't touch a paycheck anymore. Our employer dumps the numbers on our name, and off we go.

We are currency redistribution centers.

Money is energy, which we create by performing a service. For our service, we receive a statement reporting our energy gain. We can trade it in for cash but with the understanding that it is the *president's* picture on the bill and not our own. In other words, currency is vulnerable to the Have-Nots. When we buy a hamburger at McDonald's, the food is assigned a numeric value demanding a specific amount of energy. We hand over some green pieces of paper on which the energy value is recorded, and the whole lard feast is ours.

There is a vignette in the book *Jacob the Baker* that tells of a man who placed a basket of free apples on his ledge for passers-by. People strolled by and saw the apples, but stayed away. One day, the man placed a sign on the basket reading, "Delicious apples, $5 each." Soon he was swamped with people who *had* to taste a five-dollar apple.

Value is whatever we make of it. In the middle of the desert, a glass of lemonade is worth our life savings. On a deserted isle, a pot of gold is worthless. And what makes gold so precious anyway? All it does is glitter, and even then with the help of light. Gold isn't worth the paper it's printed on.

> Value is whatever we make of it.

You may have noticed the 652,741 homes burrowing into the hillsides. We have more rich people than we do hills to put them on. The land is appraised by value experts who assign long numbers to them. If we keep carving up the scenery, however, those same experts will change their minds. Or the numbers themselves may change alongside people's viewpoint.

A recession is just a rumor that other people don't have money. Wealth is just an abundance of energy. Debt is an energy imbalance. the national debt is an IOU from a guy named Franky who lost in seven-card stud and snuck out the back door.

For these reasons, I've decided to stop obsessing about the future. No more worrying about where money is coming from, what it will do when it gets here, or how I'll live when my skin shrivels. Instead, I am going to enjoy my sojourn here in the American Dream as long as it lasts. As any surfer will tell you, take what the wave gives you. I will be free with my dead presidents because, like Doritos, they'll make more. I will make more. And when someone asks me how much money I earn, I will say, "It depends on what mood I'm in."

Jason Love

GARAGE SALING

Summer is the season for baseball, barbecues, and swimming. But, in my neighborhood, it's also time to spend Saturday mornings behind an aluminum table, in the place usually reserved for the car or a dog, selling items for a quarter that you wouldn't wish on communist third world countries. I decided to have a garage sale the day I opened my closet and was nearly killed by an avalanche of five-year-old maternity clothes and a Cabbage Patch doll.

I spent a week cleaning out multitudes of baby paraphernalia and instructed my husband to sort through his dowry of rusty treasures stored in the garage since our wedding. I organized the contents of my household into three piles: used (baby accessories, birthing books, and support hose); never-been-used (electric breast pump, Thigh Master, and cookbooks with recipes that require more than five ingredients); and will-never-be-used-again (size-seven jeans, sewing machine, and anything my husband repaired).

My husband's pile consisted of an electric exit sign he found three years ago in a dumpster and a pair of crutches. I knew then it would be up to me to sell our castoffs and increase the storage space in our home.

I woke up early on Saturday morning and arranged my belongings on the driveway by dawn. Then I sat in a beach chair and waited, thinking this was the best idea I ever had because soon my closets would be uncluttered, and I wouldn't be risking my life every time I needed a sweater. I closed my eyes and dreamed about the extra storage space and cash in my future.

"Excuse me," my reverie was broken by a woman waving my son's first rattle. "How much is this?"

A vision of my son, playing with it in his bassinet, flashed through my mind.

"I'm not sure how that got out here," I said as I snatched it out of her hand and tossed it to safety behind the lawn mower, "it's not for sale."

I settled back into my chair to relax until a group of women came up the driveway and surrounded my daughter's crib like buzzards after the kill.

"How much is it?" one of them asked.

I pictured my daughter asleep and sucking her thumb safely beneath the covers. "Sorry, it's just a display," I propped the crutches up on the side and threw an outfit dating back to the Nixon administration over the top.

The morning got worse when negotiations with a six-year-old about a Barbie Camper grew more intense than the Middle East peace process; and I sold my daughter's ballet slippers and sobbed for 15 minutes over the matching leotard. I decided to quit when I sprained my back trying to hide boxes of baby clothes behind the water heater without recreating the Kent State riot in my driveway.

I closed the garage door, stumbled into the house, and collapsed on the couch. When I reached into my pocket and pulled out a handful of money, I wondered what my husband would say when he found the children's belongings hidden all over the garage.

At least I had more closet space, I thought as I crammed the money back into my pocket, *but that was the toughest eight dollars I ever made.*

Debbie Farmer

• •

The most expensive vehicle to operate, per mile, is the shopping cart.

Anonymous

• •

WHY I SHOP ONLINE

It all started with fax paper. I needed it for my now antique fax machine which I use in lieu of a copy machine. So I go to one of those warehouse-like office supply stores that could double as an aircraft hanger.

It's always a mistake for me to go to these places, because inevitably things find their way home that I never intended to buy. Paper in mesmerizing colors. Industrial-size packages of pens sporting rubbery grips that will last well into the next millennium.

Being summer, the store is like the inside of the oven. Literally. The ceiling is even covered in some kind of foil, and for a second I have one of those flashes where you temporarily forget where you are and imagine yourself doing the backstroke in au jus, then snuggling up to a potato as if it was a life preserver. I have a sudden craving for a sprig of parsley. Surely that happens to you all the time, too.

I find the fax paper (quite a feat without a Sherpa), then manage to find my way back to civilization—or at least the cash register.

While waiting in a line that appears longer than Hands Across America, I'm forced to stand irresistibly close to all manner of items I don't need but will inevitably want. I find an item fitting this description—a USB extension cable. This is something I didn't even know existed before entering this oversized Easy-Bake Oven.

Suddenly I cannot live without it. I realize that this piece of plastic and metal will allow me to plug things into my USB port without having to fight my way through a jumble of cables that, in low light, can seem like all those snakes in that Indiana Jones movie. And it's on sale!

By the time I reach the register I feel like I've crossed the Sahara and am so parched I would actually consider drinking a Mountain Dew. The only explanation for this is that I am clearly half-crazed with dehydration.

So when I hand over my credit card and see that eight-dollar fax paper and a fifteen-dollar cable have magically totalled thirty-five dollars, I almost don't notice. And even though my mouth is too dry to speak, I point the cashier to the posted price. Gee, she's sorry, but she can't

> **The only explanation for this is that I am clearly half-crazed with dehydration.**

give me a refund, I'll have to trek over to customer service.

By the time the woman behind the counter gets off the phone I am now at a point where I'd actually pay for a paper cup filled with tap water. I explain the problem, walk a half mile under the broiler to where I got the cable, show her the *two* signs with the sale price, wait while she tries to explain that the signs are for a different item, even though the item number is the same and the only item in sight is the one for which I was overcharged. Then, suddenly she says, "OK, but I don't know how to fix that."

I start wondering if it's worth ten dollars to go through this. The manager arrives, tells her what to do, she takes my credit card and disappears. I wait, tempted to buy some more pens, all the while hoping she's not online buying herself airline tickets.

Then I hear her say, "Oh, no!" which is not encouraging, then "Oh, that's bad," which is even less encouraging. Finally, she comes back and explains it: She charged it. Then she credited the original charge. Then credited it a second time, then charged it again. By this time I don't know if I've gotten my ten dollars back, or if it's cost me ten dollars more.

But since a bottle of fountain pen ink is starting to look thirst-quenching, and I fear that my wife, sitting in the car in the sun, will end up unconscious or at the very least unpleasant from heat frustration I just sign the credit card receipts.

And people wonder why e-commerce keeps growing. Granted, e-commerce isn't perfect, but I have to say it's never taken me thirty minutes to check out, all the while being made to feel like a brisket.

So while e-commerce stocks tumble, and industry pundits and so called "analysts" try to proclaim that e-commerce is dead (*ABC News* even has a splashy little graphic they call the "dot com deathwatch") what's dead are the brains of those pundits. No, not all e-commerce sites will survive—not all stores or companies of any kind do.

But *your* site *can* if you sell something unique, and provide good service. You can reach more people than you ever could with a large, foil-covered barn.

Daniel (Rocky J.) Will Harris

••

People go through 3 conversions: their head, their heart, and their pocketbook. Unfortunately, not all at the same time.

Martin Luther

••

HIP-HUGGERS

Not every woman can wear this," the salesgirl says as she slips the dress out of my hands and hangs it back on the rack.

If this chick ate a grape, she'd look like a pregnant thermometer. I figure I can take her.

"Look," I say, lifting the dress back off the rack, "this ain't *Pretty Woman* and I'm not Julia Roberts."

"Too bad," the salesgirl says as she jerks the dress out of my hands and hangs it back on the rack. "Because Julia Roberts is a size 4, and so is this dress."

I can't tell you what a thrill it is to discover that I was exactly the same size as Julia Roberts—during my first week of fetal formation.

"The main problem is your hips," the salesgirl notes as she scans me up and down using a wide-angle lens. "The rest of you seems fairly normal."

According to *Cosmopolitan*, the scientific journal for women with shoulder pads for brains, I am a "pear." In layman's terms, this means I'm shaped like a wide-body travel mug.

If you go by today's fashions, women with hips are an endangered species. Someday schoolchildren will gather around my skeleton while a teacher describes that time in history when women with giant hips walked the earth.

"Maybe we could camouflage them somehow," the salesgirl says, tapping her pouty lips with her finger.

Flipping through a rack of comfort-wear, she pulls out a pair of trousers and holds them up to me. The waist is exactly the same diameter as the hips.

"Excuse me," I say. "Do I look like a boa constrictor to you?"

I have an hourglass figure. My waist is fifteen inches smaller than my hips, and my breasts are . . . Okay, so I have a three-minute egg-timer figure.

My point is, if I buy pants that fit my hips, you could park a Volkswagen in the waistband. If I buy pants that fit my waist, I have to buy two pair—one for each thigh.

> **Coming together in a Halston huddle, all the salesgirls stare at my hips like doctors conferring on how best to separate Siamese twins.**

"Look," I sigh, "surely there is something in this store I can wear."

Coming together in a Halston huddle, all the salesgirls stare at my hips like doctors conferring on how best to separate Siamese twins. "Not a thing," they finally say in unison.

"You're telling me that I'm the only woman left in this world with hips?" I demand.

"You know, they have surgery that can fix that now," the woman at the rack next to me says knowingly.

So this is what it's come to. I'm supposed to

have the meat sucked off my bones in order to attract men who are attracted to women who look like boys.

"Gimme that dress!" I growl through gritted teeth.

Grabbing the hanger off the rack, I make a dash toward the dressing room. Weaving and ducking, I knock emaciated shoppers out of the way like *Night of the Living Dead*.

Finding an open stall, I run inside, slam the door, and slide the latch. On the wall is a little sign that reads: YOU STRETCH IT, YOU BUY IT.

Kicking off my Reeboks, I drop my jeans to the floor and toss my T-shirt on the hook. Stepping into the dress, I wiggle it into position, suck my belly button to my backbone, and zip. Holding my breath, I take a long, hard look at myself in the mirror.

I'd say it was a perfect fit—if I were an Oscar Meyer wiener. Not only can you see my panty lines, you can identify most of my major organs.

Of course, none of this matters anyway. I just caught a glimpse of the price tag. I can't afford the hanger, much less the dress.

P. S. Wall

•••

People who say money can't buy happiness just don't know where to shop.

Tom Shivers

•••

4

Why Do the Rich Get Richer and I Get Poorer?

*Some folks just have the Midas touch—
everything they touch turns to gold. Then
there's the rest of us.*

THAT'S MY MONEY

In 1972 I went to work as a writer on the private staff of "the world's richest man"—oil billionaire H. L. Hunt (the H. L. stands for Haroldson Lafayette.) And it was an experience I'll never forget.

During my tenure with Mr. Hunt I had a variety of duties and privileges. And I thought you might enjoy hearing a few of them. Naturally, since Mr. Hunt was recognized as having more personal wealth than anyone else on the planet (even by his nearest financial rival, Howard Hughes), money was a huge issue on every front. And his money attracted every kind of virtue and vermin imaginable.

In addition, having that kind of wealth gave Mr. Hunt some unique perspectives on money and how to use it.

The Nickel

It was my privilege one week to fly with Mr. and Mrs. Hunt on their private Lear jet to Hollywood, California, where Mr. Hunt was scheduled to appear on *The Merv Griffin Show*. Merv was hosting a panel of millionaires and Mr. Hunt—a billionaire. Mr. Hunt was, of course, the oldest and richest of the bunch.

We stayed in the Beverly Hilton Hotel. In fact, five of us had the entire fifth floor to ourselves. I spent most of my time in the big living room of Mr. and Mrs. Hunt's suite, waiting for him to say, "Jump," so I could respond, "How high?"

One day Mr. Hunt asked me to go down to the lobby to get something for him from the gift shop, which I did. While there, I also made a small purchase for myself. And when I came back to their suite, I had a nickel in my hand—change from my purchase. So I laid it on top of the television until I could return to my own room.

In a little while, Mr. Hunt came through the room and spied the nickel. He looked at it, and then looked back at it. Finally, he said, "Now, who's money is this?"

I laughed and teased him, saying, "Now, Mr. Hunt, that's my nickel, and I need it a lot worse than you do."

He grinned and said, "Well, I'm sure that's right." And he reluctantly walked away, leaving the nickel on the TV.

I'm convinced that, if I had said, "I don't know whose money that is," he would have picked it up and put it in his pocket. In Mr. Hunt's eyes, it seemed that all money was the same, because he had so much of it.

Note that he didn't say, "Whose nickel is this?" I believe he would have asked the exact same question if there had been a hundred-dollar bill or a penny. To him, money was money.

Here's another example.

Ice Cream

One day back in Dallas, I was summoned to Mr. Hunt's big corner office. When I arrived, Himself (that's what we called him) had some money in his hand.

"Now, I'd like for you to go get me some ice cream," he said, and he handed me a one-hundred-dollar bill and a one-dollar bill.

I said, "I'll be happy to, Mr. Hunt," and I took the money and left.

In the outer office I realized that I couldn't really buy ice cream with either bill. The dollar wasn't enough, and the ice cream store couldn't cash the hundred-dollar bill, because it was too large. I had to go downstairs to the bank and get the hundred-dollar bill changed before I could get the ice cream.

Once again, to Mr. Hunt, money was money . . . of any denomination.

Tipping the Car Hop

One of the jokes in the office was about Mr. Hunt tipping the man in the parking garage for bringing his car around at the end of the day. Even though Mr. Hunt was a billionaire, he always tipped the car hop a quarter. Behind his back, Mr. Hunt's driver gave the guy five dollars, but Mr. Hunt never knew it. And if he had known it, he would probably have been incensed by his driver's extravagance.

Once in a while Mr. Hunt would realize he didn't have a quarter in his pocket. So he would stop by the office of Welch Wright, his longtime administrator, and borrow a quarter from her. She always gave him the quarter, of course. But he rarely repaid her.

She told me one day that sometimes she would check up on Himself to see if he was still as alert as he'd always been (he was eighty-three at the time). She would go to his office and say, "Mr. Hunt, may I borrow a quarter for the car hop?"

And he would always give it to her. Then she said, without fail, the next morning when he arrived at the office, and before he ever went to his office, he stopped at her office and asked for his quarter back. That's how she knew he was still doing well.

Not Worth the Worry

Mr. Hunt's wealth brought the press around on a regular basis, of course. And it was during one of those probing interviews, when reporters tried to make an aging-but-still-brilliant man into a bumbling fool, that Mr. Hunt, as usual, turned the tables on them.

He sat at his desk with a piece of paper in his left hand, his wispy white hair mussed from running his right hand through it, waving the paper to emphasize his answers to their questions.

One reporter baited Mr. Hunt about his sporty son, Lamar, who had bought the Dallas Texans professional football team a couple of years earlier and moved them to Kansas City where they became the Kansas City Chiefs. Predictably, during the transition years, his investment in the team was in the red.

The reporter said, "Mr. Hunt, Lamar has lost over a million dollars a year on a football team. Doesn't that worry you?"

Mr. Hunt paused for a moment, as if mentally calculating, and then said, "Well, the way I figure it, if Lamar lost a million dollars a year, he'd be broke in about four hundred and fifty years." (Lamar was, of course, incredibly wealthy himself.) Then Mr. Hunt grinned his "gotcha" grin, and his blue eyes twinkled with delight, as I'd seen them do so often. To the richest man in the world, a million dollars just wasn't worth the worry.

If You've Got It, Flaunt It

Mr. Hunt was a master at getting what he wanted. One incident that proved that was when we traveled to California. We walked into the lobby of the Beverly Hills Hotel and checked in at the registration desk. Mrs. Hunt and the airplane pilots went on to the rooms reserved for us on the fifth floor, but Mr. Hunt turned to me and said, "We'll talk to the bell captain now."

At the time, Mr. Hunt was recovering from recent back surgery. So he had to hold on to my arm to steady Himself, and he could just shuffle his feet along to avoid falling. To any normal observer, in his standard blue suit and bowtie, Mr. Hunt looked like anyone's little old granddaddy and anything *but* the richest man in the world.

> **Mr. Hunt looked like anyone's little old grandaddy and anything *but* the richest man in the world.**

Also, just for background, you need to know that Mr. Hunt was a politically conservative man. And he was not passive about it. In fact, he took a very proactive stance and consistently distributed political comment material both by mail and in person. So when we traveled, we always took boxes of printed literature on political topics with us. It was not unusual for Mr. Hunt, Himself, to put the material on a table in the lobby of the hotel where he was staying and to sit beside the table talking to passersby about his political views. He did not intend for this trip to be an exception.

So we approached the young man behind the stand marked "Bell Captain."

"Young man," said Mr. Hunt politely, "I'd like to put my table up in your lobby."

The young bell captain, unfortunately for him, had no idea who Mr. Hunt was, that he was personal friends with Mr. Hilton, who owned the entire chain of Hilton hotels, or that he had a standing six-foot mahogany table in the lobby of the Dallas Hilton Hotel where his materials were allowed to stay permanently. In fact, someone from our office went to the Hilton and replenished the materials regularly.

So the bell captain responded politely, "Well, I'm sorry, sir, but there's a convention in the hotel, and that really won't be possible."

For about fifteen minutes, Mr. Hunt continued to patiently explain to the young man that it would surely be in his best interest to allow us to put up his table. And for fifteen minutes the young man continued to politely refuse. Meanwhile, I'm standing there, judiciously keeping my mouth shut and thinking, *This should be interesting!*

Finally, Mr. Hunt said, "We'll go to our room now."

I simply said, "Yes, sir." And we turned and walked to the elevator as I was thinking, *This should really be interesting.*

Once in Mr. Hunt's suite, he said to me, "Now, get me Hiltie on the phone."

I dialed the number for Mr. Hilton's Dallas headquarters, asked for Mr. Hilton's secretary, and told her Mr. Hunt wanted to speak to her boss. Instantly Mr. Hilton came on the line.

"Mr. Hilton," I said, "I have Mr. Hunt for you."

"Well, put him on!"

I handed Mr. Hunt the phone, saying, "It's Mr. Hilton."

With no greeting or small talk, Mr. Hunt said, "Hilt, I'm in your hotel out here in California, and they won't let me put my table up in the lobby."

I turned toward the window to keep from laughing, thinking, *Yep, this is going to be very interesting.* Of course, I could only hear Mr. Hunt's side of the conversation, so I don't know what Mr. Hilton said. The next thing I heard was this:

"Now, Hilt, you know I've been known to buy hotels." Click! Mr. Hunt hung up.

I almost choked to keep from laughing out loud.

In less than five minutes, there was a knock on the door. I opened the door, and there stood a very red-faced bell captain.

"Mr. Hunt, we have your table up in the lobby!"

I learned some great lessons about money from the world's richest man. And they have served me well through the years.

Mary Hollingsworth

....

A study of economics usually reveals that the best time to buy anything is last year.

Marty Allen

....

∙∙

The pastor of my church hates to plead for money. But when the coffers were running low, he had no choice.

"There's good news and there's bad news," he told the congregation. "The good news is that we have more than enough money for all the current and future needs of the parish. The bad news is, it's still in your pockets."

Giles V. Schmitt

∙∙

GOOD HABITS

I always had a nickel or a dime to put in the collection plate when I was growing up. It didn't add much to the building fund or the current expenses, but it created a habit in me that has lasted a lifetime. I feel guilty if a collection passes me and I don't add something to it. In my home church I always have an envelope to place in the plate. If I'm visiting a church somewhere else in the world, I always make sure I have extra money in my pocket for the offering just like I make sure I have extra money for popcorn when I go to the movies. I'd feel like a freeloader if I didn't add my "two-cents worth."

I have a friend, Bobby, who is an elder in our church today, who tells a wonderful story I'd love to claim as mine own, but I won't do that to him. He was eight years old or so and he and his family would walk the two blocks to church. He always passed a little store that was open on Sunday because the owners were Seventh Day Adventists. He would sneak in the store with some lame excuse each Sunday morning and buy a candy bar with the dime his mother always gave him for Sunday school. Then before Sunday school started, he and another eight-year-old friend, Skipper, would go out behind the church, break the candy bar in half and he'd sell half of it to Skipper for a dime. Skipper could afford the inflated price and never questioned it, as there was no place else to get half a Hershey bar at 10 a.m. on a Sunday morning. (Sort of like that popcorn in the movies I was talking about. You'll pay any price they want cause it's the only game in town at the time.) A lesson in basic economics will show you that this was a good deal for Bobby. He got his dime back and still got to eat half a Hershey.

> **He got his dime back and still got to eat half a Hershey.**

And this was all well and good for as long as it lasted. Except the inevitable finally happened. One Sunday morning, Skipper didn't show up for church. Family vacation, summer camp, the flu. Whatever the reason, no Skipper, and Bobby is stuck with a candy bar and no money to put in the Sunday school plate. He panicked because he was sure his teacher would rat on him to his mother that he didn't put any money in the little basket when it was passed around.

He lived in fear all that morning and all that day and all that week, just waiting for something to be said. Fortunately for him, nothing was noticed and nothing ever happened, but he learned a lesson about gambling at an early age that has stuck with him until this very day.

Money has always been a big part of the church. Until you serve on a board of deacons or a session or a council of some sort, you never realize just how much business goes on in a church. You never realize how much it takes to just pay the bills. Sometimes the business of it all gets in the way of the spiritual and you have to step back and maybe even step down for a year or so to get your perspectives in the right places again.

Jesus knew how hard it was for money and church to mix and keep an honest tone to it. He went in and turned over the tables of the moneychangers to show His anger and concern.

But at the same time there were rich women who traveled with Him and His disciples who gave money to their cause just to keep them going. His band of apostles even had a treasurer who carried the moneybag. Of course, that treasurer was named Judas and money turned out to be the last of his problems.

My daddy had a favorite old hymn he used to sing to himself while he was driving or working in the garden or just sitting in the back yard on a summer night. The song had a financial theme along with the religious message, and it comes to mind now with some words of advice he gave me in his last years concerning the church and money. He told me, "Son, always remember the more you give, the more you'll receive."

He went on to explain that that should never be the reason for the giving, but that it would be the result of the giving. He was a wise man. That was over 35 years ago and I still miss him today as if I just saw him last night. And sometimes I do see him, sitting in the back yard on a summer night.

> *Long ago (down on my knees),*
> *Long ago (I settled it all),*
> *Yes, the old account was settled long ago.*
> *And the record's clear today,*
> *For he washed my sin away,*
> *When the old account was settled long ago.*
>
> *Don Reid*

•••

Who is rich? He that is content. Who is that? Nobody.

Benjamin Franklin

•••

WHAT DO YOU SEE?

An old, rich man with a cranky, miserable attitude visited a rabbi who lived a simple life. They weren't together very long before the rabbi got a wonderful idea on how to illustrate to the man that his cranky attitude was wrong. He took him by the hand and led him over to his window and he said, "Now look out the window and tell me what you see."

As the man stood there, he said, "Well, I see some men and some women and I see a few children."

"Fine."

The rabbi then took him by the hand and led him across the room to a mirror.

"Now, look and tell me what you see."

The man frowned and said, "Well, obviously I see myself."

"Interesting," the rabbi replied. "In the window there is glass, in the mirror there is glass, but the glass of the mirror is covered with a little bit of silver. And no sooner is the silver added than you cease to see others, only yourself."

Author Unknown

••

Make sure you don't end up the richest person in the cemetery. You can't do business from there.

Colonel Sanders

••

THAT'S HOW IT IS

Our For What It's Worth Department hears from Hershey, Pennsylvania—where the woman in the Mercedes had been waiting patiently for a parking place to open up.

The shopping mall was crowded.

The woman in the Mercedes zigzagged between rows—then up ahead she saw a man with a load of packages head for his car.

She drove up and parked behind him and waited while he opened his trunk and loaded it with packages.

Finally he got in his car and backed out of the stall.

But before the woman in the Mercedes could drive into the parking space . . .

A young man in a shiny new Corvette zipped past and around her and HE pulled into the empty space and got out and started walking away.

"Hey!" shouted the woman in the Mercedes. "I've been waiting for that parking place!"

The college-ager responded, "Sorry, lady; that's how it is when you're young and quick."

At that instant she put her Mercedes in gear, floorboarded it, and crashed into and crushed the right rear fender and corner panel of the flashy new Corvette.

Now the young man is jumping up and down shouting, "You can't do that!"

The lady in the Mercedes said, "That's how it is when you're old and rich!"

Paul Harvey Jr.

· ·

You spend a billion here and a billion there. Sooner or later it adds up to real money.

Senator Everett Dirkson

· ·

••

Wife: I'm happy to see that the neighbors finally returned our lawn mower before they moved. They certainly had it long enough.

Husband: Our lawn mower? I just bought it at the garage sale they're having.

Bob Phillips

What we hate about inflation is that it didn't hit years ago when prices were lower.

Tal D. Bonham

••

OPIE AND HIS MERRY MEN

A re any of you boys rich?" the hobo asks Opie and his friends. The reaction the boys give is a little odd. In fact, none of the four boys have an answer. There are no positive or negative responses. They shrug their shoulders and say they don't know. They don't know if they are rich or not.

That was a very small scene in the episode "Opie and His Merry Men" but I thought it was interesting. At this point in the series, Opie and his friends seem to be around twelve years old. They have been running around in the woods play-ing "Robin Hood" when they come across Willie, a hobo who has set up camp nearby. It seems that Willie is down on his luck because of all the injustice that life has dealt him. He can't work because he has a bad leg from saving the life of a baby who was about to be run over by a train. Willie con-vinces the boys that it is their duty as disciples of Robin Hood to steal from the rich and give to the poor, and of course, Willie is poor. The boys are happy to oblige Willie by giving him things they take from home, but soon the boys' parents begin to notice the missing items.

Opie is a little confused by the whole situation. He asks why some people have everything they need while others have nothing. He just doesn't think it's fair that some people have to struggle just to make ends meet. When Andy finds out what the boys are doing, he reminds them that stealing is stealing and what they are doing is wrong, regardless of their good intentions. Opie asks Andy how it can be wrong if Willie can't help himself. Andy takes this opportunity to show the boys that Willie isn't quite as helpless as he claims to be. When Andy offers Willie a job and a place to stay, the hobo hightails it out of there, bad leg and all. It's now obvious that Willie is a freeloader, a lesson not lost on Opie and his friends.

During the episode, Opie asks Andy and Aunt Bee if they are rich. At first Andy says no, that you can't get rich on a sheriff's salary. Barney pipes in by saying that if you do, you're sure to be investigated! After Andy thinks for a minute, he dismisses their material wealth and remembers the other things. Andy tells Opie that their basic needs are being met, such as having a roof over their heads and plenty of food to eat. He mentions family and the fact that Andy, Opie, and Aunt Bee have each other. He also mentions that they are blessed with good friends like Barney. Opie begins to realize how much they do have to be thankful for and that, yes, they are indeed rich.

Joey Fann

....

A loan company is a place where you can borrow enough money to get you completely out of debt.

Evan Esar

....

••

Amazing, isn't it? We spend our whole lives building up money for retirement, then we die and someone else gets to spend it.

Mary Hollingsworth

Nowadays you can't live on love—without refinancing.

Evan Esar

••

TAX PREPARATION SERVICE

"Why, I couldn't have done a better job myself — that'll be $750.00."

BIG THANKS FOR SMALL FAVORS

Thank you," the woman said, following him to the van. "Thank you so much!"

"Sure," Steve said. He had just gotten his permit and had hoped he could drive home from the store, but now it just seemed too trifling to bring up.

"What was that about?" his mom asked, once the door was shut.

"It was no big deal."

"You must have done something to invoke that kind of response," she said.

"It was just a little bitty thing. I was waiting in line to pay for the milk and this little kid walked up to the candy rack and just stared at it with tears in his eyes."

"What happened?"

"His mom walked up with a couple more kids and I could see that they were really, really poor. All of a sudden his mom whispers, 'Honey, you know I would buy you a candy bar if I had the money.'"

"Then what?" his mom was tearing up too.

"I slipped a ten-dollar bill into the little guy's pocket and said, 'Hey, dude, get everyone in the family a candy bar, okay?'"

"No wonder his mom felt such gratitude!"

"Really, it was nothing, Mom."

"To you, maybe . . ." she smiled. "But to me, you're a champion! By the way, you want to drive home?"

"Oh, thank you," he said. "Thank you so much!"

A great big thank you for a little bitty thing goes a long, long way in the heart.

Heavenly Father,

I admit, sometimes I find it hard to give. I want to be generous with others, but after I've spent the entire day laying my life down for my family and taking care of all my responsibilities, I feel that there is very little left over to offer others. I certainly don't want to be stingy or selfish with my time, my energy, or my finances, because that is the opposite of Your nature. Your generosity never ceases; I want to be like You.

Make me aware of opportunities where I can do something

to make a difference. Whether it is donating canned goods to a food drive or simply helping an elderly person carry her packages into the post office, show me ways in which I can be generous with others and allow Your love to flow through me. Thank You for helping me to become the "cheerful giver" whom Your Word says You love.

Amen.

David Bordon and Tom Winters

••

Beverly Hills is so exclusive—it's the only town in America where Taco Bell has an unlisted number. And so rich—it's the only place I've seen a Salvation Army Band with a string section.

Aaron Cohl

Money is a good servant but a bad master.

Bob Phillips

••

WEALTH CANNOT BUY HAPPINESS

Whoever loves money
   will never have enough money;
Whoever loves wealth
   will not be satisfied with it.
   This is also useless.
The more wealth people have,
   the more friends they have to help spend it.
So what do people really gain?

They gain nothing except to look at
    their riches.
Those who work hard sleep in peace;
    it is not important if they eat little or much.
But rich people worry about their wealth
    and cannot sleep.

I have seen real misery here on earth:
Money saved is a curse to its owners.
    They lose it all in a bad deal
and have nothing to give to their children.
People come into this world with nothing,
    and when they die they leave with
        nothing.
In spite of all their hard work,
    they leave just as they came.
This, too, is real misery:
They leave just as they came.
    So what do they gain from chasing
        the wind?
All they get are days full of sadness
    and sorrow,
        and they end up sick, defeated,
        and angry.

I have seen what is best for people here on earth. They should eat and drink and enjoy their work, because the life God has given them on earth is short. God gives some people the ability to enjoy the wealth and prosperity he gives them, as well as the ability to accept their state in life and enjoy their work. They do not worry about how short life is, because God keeps them bushy with what they love to do.

Ecclesiastes 5:10–20

"I'm not a machine, Deborah.
I can't just turn my greed on and off."

GOOD JOB!

"Dad, can you take me to apply for a job?" asked Brad, newly sixteen.

I glanced at his fashionable interview attire, consisting of a T-shirt, board shorts, and sneakers with untied laces.

"Do you want to just apply for a job, or actually get one?" I replied.

"Huh?"

"No employer is going to hire you if you're dressed like a beach bum," I said.

"But I'm applying at Jamba Juice. Everyone there wears shorts and a T-shirt," Brad noted.

"They may let you dress that way once they hire you, but trust me, the boss will take you more seriously if you dress professionally for the interview," I said.

"When you say 'professionally,' you don't mean like *you*, do you?" he replied with raw panic in his voice. "I don't want to look like a dork!"

"And just what is *that* supposed to mean?" I snorted.

"It's not an insult," Brad replied, rushing to repair the damage. "I mean, see, it's OK for you to dress like a dork because everyone expects it, but there's no way that I—"

"Thanks for clarifying that," I interrupted. "And just what is wrong with the way I dress?"

Brad glanced down at my polished burgundy wing-tipped shoes.

"Well, for starters—" he replied.

"Never mind!" I snapped. "The point is that the person doing the hiring is not going to be a teenager. It will be someone who dresses like me, and we dorks like to hire other people who dress like dorks. Trust me on this."

"I'll wear a dress shirt, not tucked in, and no tie," he offered.

"You'll look like Oscar Madison," I replied. "You need a dress shirt, tucked in, with a tie, and I'll even loan you my wing tips."

That last part was purely for shock value, to make the tie seem easy by comparison.

Brad emerged from his room ten minutes later looking very dapper in his black slacks, gray shirt (tucked in), and deep maroon tie.

"You look great," I offered.

"If anyone sees me, I'll move to another town," he replied.

We got in the car and made our way toward the juice bar.

"Have you thought about what to say?" I asked.

"What do you mean?"

"The first question the guy is going to ask you is 'Why do you want to work here?'" I said.

"You can't know what he's going to say," Brad retorted.

"It's standard," I said. "So let's practice your answer."

"I want to earn money," Brad replied.

"Wrong," I said.

"How can it be wrong? That's why anyone wants a job!" Brad replied.

"They already know you want to earn money. But that is a boring and unimaginative answer," I said. "How did you even think to apply at this place? Why didn't you apply somewhere else?"

"Well, I went to a Jamba Juice in Sacramento and I really like their drinks, and it seems like a fun place to work," Brad said.

"Then that's your answer," I said as we drove into the parking lot.

Fifteen minutes later . . .

Brad floated out the door and toward the car.

"I start Wednesday," he said.

"Congratulations!" I said, extending my palm for a high five.

"What was his first question?" I asked.

"'So, Brad, why do you want to work here?'" Brad grinned.

"So was I right or was I right?" I gloated.

"You were right," he agreed.

"Does the old man know what he is talking about?" I prodded.

"Yeah," Brad acquiesced.

"So, am I one cool dude or what?"

Brad glanced down at my shoes.

"Let's not push it," he advised.

Dave Meurer

COUPON MOM

If you watch *Good Morning America*, you know me as the Coupon Mom. And you know that I love saving money—and I really love coupons. You find them everywhere—in newspapers, circulars, even on the Internet. I use them to buy healthy, delicious food for my family—and for my local food pantry too. I've saved thousands of dollars on groceries. So maybe you think I was raised this way. You'd be wrong. Never in a million years could I have guessed that I'd become the Coupon Mom. It's a pretty good story.

Twelve years ago my husband, Dave, and I had grueling work schedules, but we longed to start a family. Just before our first son, David, Jr., was born, I thought I had it all figured out: I'd return to work after three months, hire a sitter and keep climbing the corporate ladder.

The first time I held my newborn son in my arms, though, I realized it wasn't going to be so easy. How I wanted to watch this baby grow up! Right there at the hospital I thought, *I'm going to quit my job. But how? How could I cut our household income in half now; how would we make ends meet?*

"We'll find a way," Dave said.

I resigned from my job, excited to start my new career as a stay-at-home mom. While David, Jr., napped, I read every book on frugal living I could get my hands on. I prayed too. God new how much it meant to me to be at home. Please, Lord, you've got to help me make this work.

Some things could not be changed. We couldn't adjust our mortgage. We couldn't give up our car. But one area where we could cut costs jumped out: groceries. I was blown away by what I read in my research. "Did you know some families spend twelve hundred dollars a month on groceries," I asked Dave incredulously one night, "while others spend two hundred dollars on the exact same stuff?" How did they do it?

I started collecting the flyers that arrived with our news-paper. I figured you could save ten cents here and fifty cents there. Small change. But one Saturday I got out my calculator and shopping list and started adding things up—coupons for macaroni, diapers, cereal—crossing things off one at a time. I almost woke David, Jr., up from his nap. I wanted to shout out loud, "Do you realize that with these coupons, coupled with the store's double-coupon offer, we can save seventy-five dollars on our next trip to the store?"

I'll never forget the first time I hit the supermarket armed with my newfound weapon: a purse full of coupons. People say they feel embarrassed to use them. You know how I felt? Smart—and empowered. I'd cut my grocery bill in half.

"Steph, how will you find the food you like with coupons?" my mom asked. I reassured her: saving money on groceries isn't about changing the way you eat. It's about changing the way you buy the food you like. We still eat our favorites—great salads, roast chicken, you name it—but at a fraction of the cost. And I've learned how to be flexible about brands. Why pay more for a certain brand of peanut butter just because it's what you've always had, when another brand is just as good and a lot cheaper?

Soon, our second son, Christopher, was born. My life was busy. Sometimes I missed my old corporate job, but mostly I felt blessed to be there for David, Jr., and Christopher. From their seats in the shopping cart, they were my coconspirators, young David waving coupons that I asked him to hold.

One Sunday Dave and I were in church, waiting for the service to begin. I flipped through the bulletin. A little slip of paper caught my eye. "The Food Pantry Needs Your Help!" it read, with a Bible verse, "He that giveth to the poor shall not lack," and an address where donations could be dropped off. There was even a list of needs—mostly nonperishable items like canned soups and beans. I'll do it with coupons, I said to myself.

I hightailed it to the supermarket that week. "I got that pantry sixty dollars worth of food," I said to Dave, "for fifteen bucks!" I made an appointment with the food-pantry director. I wasn't just going to drop off a few bags of canned goods. I was going to tell her how I managed to buy all that food for so little money.

I arrived at the food pantry in my usual daily uniform: sweats and a T-shirt. I handed over the groceries, then took a seat in the small basement waiting room until the director was ready to meet with me. There was a lady sitting across from me in a dress and heels. A client. She was about my age. She looked like any other hardworking mom, trying to do the best she could for her family. *She probably had to run here on her lunch break*, I thought. Or on her way to work after dropping her kids off at daycare. Then something happened that I will never forget: she looked across the room and flashed the warmest, kindest smile I'd ever seen. *She thinks I'm a new client!* I thought. *She wanted me to know I would be okay.*

I looked over and saw a man in blue jeans and a sweatshirt pick up some of the food I'd just delivered. The food I'd bought with coupons. It had hardly cost me anything, and because of it this man and his family would have a good dinner tonight. I decided I'd start buying food for charity every week with my unused coupons. I called up my mom and told her about the food pantry. It made me angry that in our affluent area there were all these people struggling just to make ends meet.

"Steph, do you think you could teach this to other people?" Mom asked. "How to buy food with coupons? For their own families, and to help folks out?"

"I don't know," I said. "People think I'm a little weird with my coupons as it is."

Mom was silent for a moment. "Why don't you pray about it?" she said. "Then invite a few friends over for coffee and ask if they'll buy food for the pantry too."

As usual, Mom knows best. I prayed, "Lord, please don't let them think I'm crazy!" I invited three friends, as a start. Not only did they not think I was crazy—soon they were teaching their friends, and we built up a network of thirty-five shoppers buying food for themselves and for charity!

That was five years ago. I wrote a book, *Greatest Secrets of the Coupon Mom*, went on TV and started a Web site. I show people how they can save money and how they can give to others by using coupons. They're both part of living a good life: saving and giving. When we give to the poor, we do not lack. We share God's abundance. And that's a pretty good story too.

Stephanie Nelson

....

A penny saved is a penny earned.

Benjamin Franklin

....

NEVER UNDERESTIMATE THE POWER OF A PENNY

Most would agree that being a mother of two active boys is both a blessing and challenge. As a stay-at-home mom, I embraced this concept by constantly thanking God for my sons, while at the same time, keeping a constant watch over their busy and curious minds.

So determined was I to keep them safe and to teach them well, that I didn't leave my boys alone for a moment . . . not even to use the restroom! However, since my thirteen-month-old baby, Paul, was happily playing in the hallway outside our bathroom door and Jerome, who was then four years old, was not far from him playing with his cars on the tiled hall floor, I decided to use the opportunity to take a much needed trip to the bathroom. I left the bathroom door open, of course!

While in there taking my very welcomed, but small break, I took a moment to run my hands down my face and blew out a sigh. As I reached for the toilet paper, I heard a very loud electrical pop! A huge flash of fire knocked Paul back and over. I rushed over to him, swept him up into my arms, and ran back to the toilet seat so I could allay the damages. He didn't have a scratch or burn on him. Not a hair, not an eyelash. Nothing. He grinned at me. I looked out the bathroom door to see the wall above the hallway nightlight completely charred, the wallpaper ruined.

Jerome came running into the bathroom at that moment and said, "What happened?"

I said, "I don't know!" and kept crooning to Paul and asking him if he was okay.

It was then that I noticed that Jerome was grinning from ear to ear, and trying to stifle his laugh by covering his mouth. Normally, his actions would have made me laugh, but at that moment, I was not amused and scolded him.

"What's so funny, young man? Your brother could have been killed!"

Poor Jerome's face became very repentant at my scolding and he said, "I'm sorry, Mommy, but it did look kinda funny when you ran with your unnerwears down."

I stopped for just a second and thought about the scene Jerome had just witnessed—me running a rescue with my pants down. I began to laugh with Jerome. Paul, thinking he did something wonderful, clapped his chubby hands and joined in giggling with us.

When I went over to survey the damages of the blackened wall, I gingerly and cautiously pulled the nightlight out of the socket. There, with two lines burnt completely through, was a penny. Apparently, Paul had discovered a new place for pennies

. . . behind the nightlight! Every single other outlet in my house was protected with child guards except for the hallway one, which was covered with the nightlight.

With this incident I have learned two concepts . . . that guardian angels are *real*, and can protect my children better than I can, and never underestimate the power of something so seemingly insignificant as a penny.

Elizabeth Schmeidler

. . . .

A man there was, and they called him mad; the more he gave, the more he had.

John Bunyan

. . . .

THE MIGHTY EMU

I've been thinking about emus," Charlie says.

"Emus." I nod. "Aren't they like big chickens?"

Charlie and I used to work together. Every couple of months or so he swings through town and buys my lunch, compliments of his company credit card.

"Emus are really up and coming," Charlie says, checking for red as he slices into the slab of prime rib flopped across his plate.

"They sell emu futures?" I ask, buttering a roll.

"Nope," he says, pointing his fork at me. "I'm going to quit my job and grow them."

From engineer to chicken farmer . . . movin' on up!

There comes a time in everyone's life when you wake up and say to yourself, "This isn't a job—it's hell with a benefit package."

"Charlie," I say, crunching on a cucumber, "have you ever seen an emu?"

Once you've made the decision to move on, you instantly develop the short-timer's attitude. With a smirk on your face, you glance around at your coworkers and think, Looo-sers.

"Wasn't that an emu in *Green Eggs and Ham*?" I ask.

You're charged with the exhilaration of change. Your possibilities are limitless, but you're not fussy. As long as there's international travel, a company credit card, and unlimited golf involved, you could be happy.

"They're very docile," Charlie says as he whips out a brochure:

Emus—Your Path to Financial Independence.

You're a humble person by nature, but a prestigious title would be nice—perhaps something like "Chancellor of the Exchequer."

"Definitely docile," I say, staring into the beady eyes of an 8 1/2 x 11 full-color glossy emu.

You call up the guy at the employment agency and inform him that this is his lucky day. You've decided to change careers—something different, new, exciting—maybe something that would benefit mankind. There's a long pause on the phone . . . followed by a dial tone.

"Charlie," I say, "do they allow emus at your condo?"

You pick up the Sunday paper, comb through the want ads and come to the rather stark realization that if you were to leave your current position, you might actually have to work for a living.

"Fillet emu," I say.

"It could happen," Charlie says.

You network all your networks, contact all your contacts, and work all your coworkers and are dismayed to discover they're hoping you're calling to offer them a better job.

"Wow, I had no idea an emu could run forty miles per hour," I say, reading the brochure.

You dust off your résumé and it disintegrates in your hands.

"... And they produce five pounds of manure per day— *each.*"

You begin to have the nagging suspicion that you're not really qualified to do anything. In fact, you're pretty sure you couldn't get the job you've got now.

"Charlie," I say, "how many emus do you suppose it's going to take to make a mortgage payment and two car payments and put three kids through college?"

"I can't take it anymore," Charlie whimpers.

"I know," I say, patting his hand. "But, honey, the only thing you know how to grow is hair."

And frankly, my little emu, that's not thriving like it used to.

P. S. Wall

• •

Beware of little expenses. A small leak will sink a great ship.

Benjamin Franklin

When it comes to money, your *yearning* power will always exceed your *earning* power.

Rick Atchley

• •

5

Wooden Nickels and Plastic Cash

My mom used to say, "Don't take any wooden nickels!" So, today, instead we happily accept plastic cash. Do you see a pattern here?

SOUND FISCAL PLANNING
(AND OTHER QUAINT MYTHS)

"Money management" is a vitally important life skill to learn and to pass on to your children, and with thoughtful planning and discipline it can be surprisingly simple to implement as long as you are the king of Switzerland. For those of us who are not rulers of wealthy nations, "money management" is a myth right up there with Big Foot and alien abductions (but less believable).

I absolutely loathe money-management lectures, workbooks, charts, videotapes, and assorted paraphernalia, and I *especially* loathe the finger-pointing, bean-counting, sanctimonious little

"I'm-more-prudent-than-you" accountant trolls who make me feel dense and guilty and irresponsible and doomed. If I sound a little testy, it is only because I am writing this late at night after I have just paid all the bills. The only money I have left to "manage" is the change in the ashtray of my aging Ford station wagon. One dollar and sixty-seven cents, to be exact.

According to the money-management experts, at this point in my life I should have a balanced portfolio consisting of mutual funds, growth stocks, and six months' worth of income invested in a readily accessible "liquid" account.

I don't.

Rather, I have invested heavily in orthodontic services, Froot Loops, and my boys' basketball shoes.

But the smug little trolls, on the other hand, are all mailing sizable checks each month to investment companies like "Mutually prudent People Who Live in Omaha." All of the mutually prudent people live in Omah, where there is really nothing to do with your money except purchase wheat by the boxcar. Once the novelty of that wears off, they amass large quantities of cash, which they cram into grain elevators until there is no more room. They finally resort to lending excess loot to people like me in the form of VISA cards with exorbitant interest rates.

> **Rather, I have invested heavily in orthodontic services, Froot Loops, and my boys' basketball shoes.**

I used to sort of admire the fiscally prudent people, with their foresight and self-restraint and plans for the future. But that was before I realized that there are no "Six Flags Over the Wheat Fields" theme parks, or anything *else* to spend money on in the grain-infested state of Nebraska. So it isn't like they are really any better or smarter than the rest of us; it's just that they don't have a lot of material temptations in Omaha.

But making fun of financially secure people will not change the fact that my own finances are hardly in stellar shape. I would feel guilty enough if I were alone in this mess, but I am a parent and I am supposed to be modeling all kinds of virtues for my boys, including financial responsibility.

For a long time I tried to fake fiscal responsibility in the expectation of eventually achieving it, desperately hoping that no one would catch on before I succeeded in getting my fiscal house in order. (Hey, Congress got away with this for *years.*)

But fakery has its limits, especially as your kids get older and start wising up.

Me: "Mark, let's discuss prudent financial management today. The habits you make here and now will serve as the foundation for your financial future. Let's do a role play; I'll pretend to be the customer and you will be the lending institution."

Mark: "Let me guess. You need gas money again until you get paid."

Me: "Ha, ha, ha! What a jokester! This is a training exercise for *your* benefit, you little comedian."

Mark: "It will cost you 30 percent interest, compounded daily."

Me: "That's highway robbery! Not even Louie the loan shark charges that much! I checked!"

Mark: "Hey, anyone who needs to consistently borrow money from a minor is a credit risk. I figure I am doing you a favor at anything less than a rate of 50 percent. Pay me back by next week or I'll report your account as delinquent."

Me: "You know, Jesus drove people like you out of the temple with a whip."

Mark: "I donate a percentage of the profits I make off you to the church. How else do you think they could have funded the remodeling of the youth center? Talk about a win-win situation."

Providing this kind of "hands-on" training in money management can help your children grasp the importance of
financial planning.

I call it "Reverse Illustration."

"Don't be like me, and one day you could be the king of
Switzerland" is the message I give my children.

Maybe they will be so grateful that they will let me live
with them someday in their spacious mansions in Nebraska.

Dave Meurer

••

**A generous man will prosper; he who refreshes
others will himself be refreshed.**

Proverbs 11:25

••

THE WRONG PRICES

In the city of Philadelphia, the night before Halloween is
always designated Mischief Night. You can imagine what
bad little boys do on that particular evening.

Two of us broke into a five-and-dime not far from my
house. We didn't steal anything. We did something far worse.
We went around and changed the price tags on just about
everything in the store. The next morning, people found that
radios were selling for ten cents apiece, while bobby pins were
priced at ten dollars. What was valuable had been made
cheap, and what was cheap had been made valuable.

That story is indicative of what has happened to America.
It is almost as though someone has broken into our society
and changed the price tags. We are not willing to invest very
much in what is really precious, and we seem to spend all of

our time and energies on that which is worthless. Our values are all mixed up!

Tony Campolo

"I sold it!"

. . . .

The safest place to double your money is to fold it over once and keep it in your pocket!

Kathleen Russell

. . . .

DEAR CARDHOLDER: FRANKLY, WE EXPECTED BETTER OF YOU

Dear Valued Credit Card Holder:

One year ago we welcomed you to the EASY COME EASY Go ("ECEG") Credit Card Family with open pockets and the kind of unbeatable terms we could offer to only a select few. As you will recall, our unparalleled benefits included the following Preferred Customer Perks:

a. A generous rebate program;

b. Triple or nothing warranty deals;

c. Frequent flyer points for your pets; and

Our weekly ECEG-Picks Lottery (ECEG employees and their families not eligible to participate, lottery not available where prohibited by law, ECEG-Picks temporarily inactive due to pending class action suit).

You will also recall that you received our special, one time only, introductory interest rate—the one that drove our Chief Financial Officer to drink. You also received our personal guaranty that our rates would never exceed those of any credit company under federal investigation.

So it is with deep regret and sadness that we advise you of our disappointment with you as a customer. Yes, disappointment. For despite our unmatched terms, you have not met your end of the bargain. Not only have you failed to use your card more than three times during the last twelve months, but on each occasion, you paid your bill in full and on time. This is inconsistent with your prior credit history, and frankly, we expected better of you.

Your prompt payments and inadequate use of your credit card force us to take the drastic action of converting your account to Non-Preferred Customer Status.

Your prompt payments and inadequate use of your credit card force us to take the drastic action of converting your account to Non-Preferred Customer Status. As a Non-Preferred Customer, you will be assessed a ten dollar carrying charge for each month in which you fail to use your card and a five dollar surcharge on each paid-on-time monthly bill. Additionally, your Preferred Customer Perks will be eliminated, except for our rebate program which will henceforth be limited to purchases made in Venezuela.

To avoid a $50 penalty, kindly turn in your Platinum Preferred Customer Card in person within one week. At that time you will be given an ugly brown card bearing the words "NON-PREFERRED" in bold letters. (Consult the enclosure to find a Card Exchange Site conveniently located no more than 120 miles from your home.)

We are pleased to report that your Non-Preferred Status will not prevent you from purchasing an unlimited number of Easy Come Easy Go tee shirts at a bargain price of $19.95 plus tax and $5 shipping.

Moreover, if you act quickly you can still qualify for Preferred Customer reinstatement. Simply use your card at least 12 times in the next 3 months, incur debt in the minimum sum of $3,000, and pay no more than 10 percent of the amount owed on your card each month plus interest. Yes, that's all it takes to re-qualify for Easy Come Easy Go's Preferred Customer Perks.

Thank you for doing business with EASY COME, EASY GO, and HAPPY SHOPPING!

> Sincerely,
> Frank N. Simseer, Jr., President
> EASY COME EASY GO Credit Services

Madeleine Begun Kane

· ·

The only reason a great many American families don't own an elephant is that they have never been offered an elephant for a dollar down and easy weekly payments.

Author Unknown

· ·

SHIPWRECKED

Two ladies were shipwrecked on an island. One lay against a palm tree, calm and serene. The other stood screaming, "We're going to die! There's no food, no water, no shelter! Don't you understand? We're going to die!"

The first lady replied, "*You* don't understand. I make one hundred thousand dollars a week."

The second lady looked dumbfounded. "What difference does that make? We're on an island with no food or water. We're going to die!"

The first lady answered, "You just don't get it. I make one hundred thousand dollars a week and I tithe ten percent to the church. Relax! My pastor will find us!"

Pam Vredevelt

Stocks

- Many an innocent lamb is drowned in a stock pool.

- A stock market investor is someone who is alert, informed, attuned to the economic heartbeat of America, and cries a lot.

- I've been burned in the stock market by picking up a hot tip.

- I made a killing in the stock market. I shot my broker.

- A friend in need is a friend who has been playing the stock market.

- People who play the market are often led astray by false profits.

- The only difference between the current stock market and the *Titanic* is that the *Titanic* had a band.

- I'll never understand the stock market. Some of my stocks just went from the financial page to the comics.

  Bob Phillips

"All right! He found dry land <u>and</u> an ATM!"

THE RIGHT KIND OF DEBT

One day when I was about 17 and my brother, Palmer, was 19, we sought out my father—we called him Pop—while he was reading his newspaper in the living room after supper. We had something really important we wanted to talk to him about. At that teenage stage of our lives, appearances were, we thought, extremely important.

Pop had this awful habit of buying a new car, usually a plain Chevrolet, about once in a blue moon and then driving it till it practically fell apart. He seemed totally unconcerned that others were buying shiny new cars every couple of years.

My brother and I decided to tell Pop that we thought it was time he bought a new car. Other kids' fathers had new cars and those other kids got to drive their fathers' new cars; we still had to drive the old Chevy.

Pop listened to what we had to say, then smiled indulgently, and said, "I can't afford a new car," and returned to his newspaper.

We weren't ready to give up. If he couldn't afford a brand-new car, maybe he could at least be persuaded to buy something newer than what we had. "Well, how about a used car?" my brother asked him.

"A used car!" he said, putting the paper down again. "Why would I want to buy a used car? I've got a used car now."

My brother was a very bright boy, but neither he nor I could refute Pop's logic. We learned to be content driving the same old used Chevy.

Over the years, we've had a lot of fun recalling that incident. Pop's remark has become sort of a famous quotation in our family. But when the laughter fades, we are struck by the wisdom of Pop's response to our wanting something we couldn't afford.

Back then, no one had heard of "money management," certainly not my brother or I. But Pop knew about managing what he had—and not worrying about things he didn't have, which would have made a very long list. He had been orphaned when he was 14 years old and had been on his own since then. Economy and thrift, making do and doing without, were subjects he, like others who had lived through hard times, knew a lot about.

In the late-Depression and World War II years of my boyhood, Pop's words made a big impression on me. Now, in this age of superabundance, my family is finding that a lot of Pop's ideas are still valid.

In fact, in today's free-spending way of life I believe Pop's frugality might actually be more valid than ever, especially for those who want reminders of what is really important in life. Refusing to keep up with the Joneses (and thus making the old Chevy do) is a money-management principle that has helped me many times since my father lived it for his kids to see.

It wasn't the only such principle that Pop and others of his generation lived by. Some of their precepts were summed up in maxims Pop used to quote to us. "Poor but honest" was one of them. "We might be poor," he'd tell my brothers and me, "but we're honest." Honesty, we learned, was like the pearl of great price, a lot more valuable than almost anything else we could wish for.

"Ragged but clean," was another of Pop's maxims. When my brother or I would point protestingly to frayed shirts or worn pants, his or ours, Pop would say, "They might be ragged, but they're clean." Clean and neat, we learned, counted for more than new and stylish.

Taking care of whatever we had, no matter how old or used, was something else we learned. "You'll never have anything," Pop would aphorize, "if you don't take care of what you've got." My own kids, now grown and two generations removed from Pop's, have themselves seen the truth of that in the lives of some of their friends, who wreck cars, ruin clothes, and neglect costly homes.

> Taking care of whatever we had, no matter how old or used, was something else we learned.

Like many of his bygone generation, Pop believed generosity was a vital part of thrift. During the 1930s, when many people were poor, including us, homeless men drifted down our street and stopped at our house, asking for something to eat. Pop met them on the front porch, told them to sit on the glider, then went into the kitchen and asked my mother to fix a meal for whoever was sitting out there. When Mama had the breakfast or dinner ready, Pop would take it out to the porch, give it to the hungry men, then sit down and talk with them while they ate it. I never saw Pop refuse anyone who asked him for help.

When he would finally get around to buying a new car, he usually gave the old one away rather than trade it in, figuring that someone needier than himself could coax a few more miles out of it.

He was able to coax financial mileage out of our house. He put three sons through college, although he had never gone himself, by borrowing against our house. For a while, my two brothers and I were all in college at the same time, and when the last of us had graduated, Pop owed more on our house than he had originally paid for it.

He never resented the damage we had done to his finances, however. In fact, he thought it was kind of a joke that he had squeezed three college educations out of one little two-bedroom house.

I've kept Pop's money-management ideas in mind and tried to apply them for nearly 40 years of coping with my own family's finances and needs. I like to think that, with the considerable help of my wife and kids, we haven't done all that bad.

We have a couple of cars, neither of them new but both of them paid for, which is, we think, still the best feature to be found in a car. We don't buy cars—or hardly anything else—unless we can pay cash for them, and so that means we drive the old ones a while after they've gone out of style. But paying cash has taught us how to save, and that's something that never goes out of style.

We have credit cards, but we use them only for convenience. We don't charge what we can't pay for in 30 days. We don't worry about keeping up with anybody. Some of our friends have a lot more than we do, but they love us anyway, just as we love our friends who have less than we do. It's the people that count, not their means.

Our fourth child graduated from college last spring, and when he did, neither he nor I owed anything for his education. Like his brothers, he had worked and saved to pay part, and I had managed to pay the rest. All of our children went to state universities, which was all we could afford but of which they are all justifiably proud because they got good educations.

I've tried to follow Pop's example of giving to worthy causes and needy people. My church gets my tithe, and the needy get whatever I can afford.

Even while trying to manage my money the best way I can, I still have a debt left over from years gone by. It's what I owe Pop and his generation for passing on to me their thrifty ways. I know that it will never be paid for completely, but by passing on thrift to my own children I hope to have repaid a small part of that debt. For those good old principles of sound management—not merely of money but of life as well—are as vital today as they ever were, and will stand our children, and their children, in good stead. Thanks, Pop. I'm indebted to you.

Benton Patterson

••

You cannot have everything. I mean, where would you put it?
Steven Wright

Once, in Juarez, Mexico, comedian Steve Martin approached a street vendor and asked the price of a broad-brimmed straw hat.

"Four dollars, señor," the man replied.

"I'll give you six dollars," Steve said.

Out of habit the vendor shot back, "For you, I make it three."

"No, I'll give you eight," Steve said.

By now the vendor was confused.

"What, señor?"

"OK," Steve said, "I'll give you ten dollars or nothing!"

The Mexican shrugged and took the money.

Rusty Wright

"We need to scale back our bathroom remodeling plans. We went over budget when I bought this pad and pen!"

The old accountant retired after fifty years, and in the top drawer of his desk they found a note that said: "Debits in the column toward the file cabinet. Credits in the column toward the window."

Brian Becker

THE ONE FOR ME

I will never forget the moment I knew that John was the one for me. It was 1981, and we were young and in love. It was October, and in Jackson, Mississippi, that means that the state fair comes to town. John and I had been dating about four months and knew that we were in love, but we had yet to determine exactly how much. I do, however, recall wanting him to kiss me almost every time I drew a breath. (If only I could muster that much emotional energy these days. Youth is, indeed, wasted on the young.)

Anyway, we went to the fair after our classes were over at Mississippi College. Oh, the smell of cotton candy, grilled onions and sausage, and caramel apples! And the *piece de resistance:* the Martha White flour biscuits and cane molasses offered for free! Sponsored by Jim Buck Ross and the Mississippi Department of Agriculture, that booth always had a half-mile-long line of people waiting to get those sweet biscuits. The biscuits are warm and tender, the molasses created that very day by mules walking around in circles, grinding up the fresh sugar cane. They pour the cane juice onto large cooking surfaces, where it's reduced to the thick, sweet, sticky bite of heaven itself.

In retrospect, I have often wondered how our young stomachs could handle all that we threw at them while wandering up and down the midway. Full of gyros and funnel cakes and having just come from the Ferris wheel (with a lovely view of downtown Jackson), we were feeling happy that we still had a few dollars in our pockets. Then the hawker invited us under his tent. His pitch: "Give me ten dollars for the chance at winning this wonderful tool set. How can you lose?" So I asked John for a ten-dollar bill and handed it to the Hawker Man. John stayed back near the edge of the tent. Within seconds, the Hawker Man gave the tool set away to another dollar contributor. Then he said, "For those of you who are left, only twenty dollars more can buy you a chance at this fab-u-lous stereo!"

Who wouldn't want to take advantage of this wonderful opportunity? Of course, I looked back at John and he handed me a twenty with a bemused expression on his face. I knew that this was a sacrifice. We were both college students, and sometimes twenty dollars was the difference between having gas and food or being immobile and hungry. As you could already guess, the stereo went to someone else. But the hawker wasn't done yet. "For only twenty dollars more, each of you can have the chance at winning the be-au-ti-ful color television set." I was in all the way now. Not that I *needed* a TV. I lived at home with my parents, and John already had one in his apartment. But I was so caught up in the moment, I just knew that it would somehow complete my life and validate that I hadn't just thrown away all the other money. I couldn't stop now. I was this close.

Besides, the odds were in my favor. Of the twenty or so people standing around handing money to this man, three had already won. And the man kept saying, "Everyone will be a winner. Everyone will win something." Those words reverberated in my head. I knew it was my time to win. I looked back at John with pleading eyes. That was his only money for the rest of the week. He knew it; I knew it. But wasn't everyone going to be a winner? He handed me his last twenty dollars and, with a slight shake of the head, drifted back to his spot toward the edge of the tent.

I eagerly handed his twenty dollars to the persuasive carnival man. I must have looked like the most eager beaver in the crowd while I waited the twenty seconds it took for him to take twenty-dollar bills from the others left standing. At this point, almost everyone had cut their losses and departed from the front area to console themselves with a Pronto Pup corn dog. I was thrilled! I now had *much* better odds at winning.

There were only a few of us remaining at the front. I was a shoo-in! I waited with bated breath as the man pulled the ticket stub from the bowl and called out a different number than mine. My heart sank. But wasn't everyone going to win *something?* The man started passing out the consolation prizes. He handed me a curio cabinet about thirty inches high and ten inches across made out of pressboard and plastic. All told, it was worth about $4.50, if that.

I looked at it, incredulous that I had just blown fifty bucks on something so lame. I was afraid to turn around and face John. I just knew he was going to have some sort of weird mix of consternation over my blowing his last dime, disappointment in my lack of ability to discern a swindle when I saw one, and general loss of faith in his new love. I teared up just thinking about the lecture formulating in his head and well deserved on my part. With a heavy heart, I turned around to face the music.

There is no rational explanation for what happened next, except that some people have a great capacity for grace. When I sheepishly searched for John's face near the back of the tent, all I could see was his neck because he had his head fully thrown back, laughing out loud. He wasn't mad. He wasn't disappointed in me. He hadn't lost faith in me. He was laughing. I knew I had found the love of my life.

That curio cabinet still hangs in our house. It is a testament to love and grace.

Anita Renfroe

. . . .

When you fix your eyes on things, invariably it leads to materialism. You fix your eyes on things and you will continually be attracted to gadgets, money, an abundance of the plastic, chrome, metal, wood, all the elements about us. You will continually be dissatisfied. The millionaire, John D. Rockefeller, was asked one time, "How much does it take to satisfy a man completely?" He said, "It takes a little bit more than he has."

Spiros Zodhiates

I often enjoy the comments made by sportsmen and women who still have a sense of humor. Lee Trevino is one of those people. He is a rather intense golfer, but he never has lost his sense of humor. He said when he was little his family was so poor that when his mother tossed the dog a bone, the dog had to call for a "fair catch" or the kids would get it.

Dennis Waitley

. . . .

CHOICES

God says, "The love of money is the root of all kinds of evil" (1 Timothy 6:10, NIV). Now some folks think that scripture means that money itself is evil, but that's not what God said. He said it's the *love* of money that causes the problems.

Money, in and of itself, isn't good or evil—it's just a medium of exchange that's more convenient to carry around than gold bars. The people using the money create the good or evil, depending on how they spend it. The more they love their money, the less they are likely to love whoever or whatever gets in their way of having more of it. It's a choice.

Just think, you can use money . . .

- To construct a tavern or a temple;
- To hurt others or to help them;
- To obliterate or beautify;
- To discourage or encourage;
- To tear down or build up;
- To create a garbage dump or a garden;
- To impress the rich or bless the poor;
- To sadden or gladden;
- To promote war or peace;
- To show hate or love.

It's a choice. A new choice every day. And through the years, the individual choices you make become the pattern of your life—a pattern for your children and grandchildren to follow. What will be the pattern of your life?

Mary Hollingsworth

● ●

It's easier to make money than to keep it.

Yiddish Proverb

● ●

"We need an exorcism. Our credit history keeps coming back to haunt us!"

WORDS THAT TRUST

The long line snaked around, like one for tickets to a rock concert in town for only one performance. The line had begun to form as early as 4:00 a.m. The draw was an opportunity to sign up for three personal fifteen-minute consultations with the agents and editors of choice at the fifth annual Maui Writers' Conference.

Maggie Bedrosian fell into line behind a particularly weary soul, a young bearded man who kept talking through his yawns. They quickly struck up a conversation and shared their life stories much like airline passengers do when they know they'll never see each other again upon arrival at their destination.

Finally, the bearded man reached the ticket desk at the head of the line. Eagerly, he pulled out his American Express card and handed it, along with the scrap of paper containing his choice of agents, to the woman behind the table.

She turned back to the man. "Sir, I'm sorry, but we don't take American Express."

"What?"

"Do you have another card we can swipe?" the woman asked, trying to be helpful.

"Oh no!" the bearded man said, clearly distressed. "How can you not take American Express?"

"Sir, there are other people waiting behind you. Do you have another card, cash, or a check?"

"No," his voice was low this time. He glanced back over his shoulder at the line that snaked about 100 yards behind him.

"You just don't understand—I've got to get these appointments. I've come all the way from North Carolina."

The clerk said, "Sir, would you step aside a moment so that—"

"Here, put it on mine," Maggie said from behind him, touching his elbow with her credit card.

He turned around and stared at her, "But you don't even know me!"

She smiled. "But I know what you've *been through*."

Dianna Booher

IF YOU CAN DREAM IT

When my sons were little and people asked them about their mom, they said, "She colors all day." Their reply still makes me laugh, because coloring is the kind of activity a lot of adults might think strange. It's right up there with dreaming. Dreaming, some think, is a waste of time.

Good thing my mom and dad didn't believe that. They had a different perspective, one they passed on to me.

My mother claims I was drawing from the time I could pick up a pencil. My early efforts weren't all that different from those of other kindergarten kids. But something happened when I was in the second grade to change all that: I got glasses. Glasses with blue frames that curved up like kittycat eyes and had sparkles in the corners. When I put them on, I couldn't believe it. "The trees have leaves!" I cried. My fuzzy world was brought into focus, and I eagerly put down the tiniest details on paper. I had so much fun that I started drawing a character who looked like me, with big glasses and short hair, often wearing hats just as I did. I called her Ann Estelle, after my maternal grandmother. And I imagined how she would go with me as I became an artist and drew pictures that made people smile.

In elementary school I had been a good student, but by high school my grades had dropped so drastically that I wasn't allowed to take art. I couldn't wait to get out of school and pursue my heart's desire—to illustrate children's books. I told that to my guidance counselor and she was appalled. "You can't do that," she said. "You've got to be practical. Get a degree in English so you can teach."

When I graduated from high school I was ready to start my life as an artist. I went to work at a local art supply store, where I learned about different media and how to use them. More important, I got to know all kinds of working artists. I realized it was possible to make a living doing what I had always wanted to do, so I soaked up as much information and advice as I could. Later, I learned a lot more at a tiny local ad agency called Hot Buttered Graphics. When the owner moved out of town, I was twenty-two and on my own. Of course there were people who thought being an artist was too unrealistic for everyday life and often asked, "So, Mary, what are you really going to do?"

When I married Phil Delano in 1977 I was working as a freelance artist, getting a little work here, a little work there. We lived from check to check on Phil's social worker's salary so I could continue to draw. But even when finances were tightest, Phil never pressured me to get a "real" job. I did feel pressured, though to go to the big city. "You can't stay here and expect to succeed," I was told. "You've got to try to sell your work in New York." I was just so hopeful that I could make it as an artist, and I felt like it was going to happen.

Phil had a friend in New York City who helped me set up some interviews with several children's book publishers. So in 1977, I anxiously took off with a bulging portfolio for the Big Apple.

Editors all liked my work, but they almost never hired free-lance or out-of-town book illustrators who didn't already have an established name. One art director, though, did suggest I try greeting cards. At the time I was kind of crushed, because I really had my heart set on illustrating children's books, and to me, greeting cards seemed like a step down.

Then I thought of my parents, and the faith they had had in me right from the beginning. I remembered when I was nine years old, and hurried home to tell Mom that I had met my first real artist. She was a woman who sometimes baby-sat for us and had her own studio set up in her basement. "Mommy," I announced, "I need a studio."

Mom didn't say, "Honey, we don't have space for you to have anything like that" (which we didn't). She merely nodded matter-of-factly as though my request made perfect sense—and emptied our linen closet. Out went the vacuum, mops, and towels, and in went my desk, chair and pen-and-ink set. I sat crammed in there for hours, learning how to draw by copying the illustrations from my mother's and grandmother's old-fashioned storybooks and signing my work with my very convenient initials, ME.

From that time on my parents always treated my art as serious business. Bolstered by their support, I continued on even without formal training, telling myself over and over what they had instilled in me: "Of course you can become an artist. Keep working for it. If you can imagine it, you can achieve it. If you can dream it, you can become it."

So, back from New York, I picked up my colored pencils and got to work. When I really thought about it, I realized my one-shot illustrations were perfect for greeting cards. At the risk of sounding like a Pollyanna, I can hardly think of a disappointment that you can't eventually turn into a good situation. So I found myself doing what I had done since childhood, illustrating those wonderful little moments of life . . . what was outside my window and inside my heart.

From all those classic children's books I had copied as a child, I had learned the technique of pulling a key line out of the text and illustrating it. Into my mind came words I had overheard long before, when a young friend was being lectured by his father. "Son," the father said grandly, "here's a lesson you might as well learn right now: Life is not just a chair of bowlies." I created a design based on this scrambled up phrase, took it to a greeting card company, and "Chair of Bowlies" became my first nationally distributed greeting card.

Excited by continuing sales, I turned to a treasure trove of quotes I had collected through the years, from philosophers, friends, and strangers. I've always been interested in what makes people act the way they do, do what they do, or say what they say. I try to put that in my cards, and to my delight, it is something that really seems to connect with people. Sometimes I quote famous people like Ralph Waldo Emerson or Marcel Proust, or I used verses from the Bible (for an upcoming book I've illustrated the Christmas story in Luke). Other times, I draw inspiration from my family or from my own life, remembering when my bossy tendencies as a child made me think "It's Good to Be Queen."

When my children were born—Evan in 1980 and Will in 1983—so was a whole new source of material. For instance, one day when Will was eight, I was feeling overwhelmed.

Sensing how flustered I was, Will tried to comfort me. "I know what's the matter, Mom," he said earnestly. "You just want a little peace of quiet." I smiled, calmed down—and used his words for my next greeting card.

My cards sold so well that in 1986 Phil and I formed our own greeting card company, and things kept growing from there. Now, in addition to greeting cards, Mary Engelbreit Studios produces calendars and books, as well as everything from figurines and jewelry to notepaper and T-shirts. We also have a national decorating magazine, *Mary Engelbreit's Home Companion*, a retail company, and even our own Web site.

Inevitably, some critics snort and say my work is too cute, too sweet, and too good to be true. They just flat out don't believe it. But what I draw is taken from my life. I had a fantastic time as a kid. So, to people who say, "You're drawing an idealized world where you'd like to live," I say, "Of course I am. What's wrong with that? Don't you wish you lived there too?"

Today my studio is only ten miles from where I was born—from where my parents encouraged a little girl to color away in a closet, to use her imagination and dream her dreams. As far as I'm concerned, dreaming isn't a pleasant pastime; it's a responsibility. We all have to do it, to bring a sense of fun and wonder into our daily lives. And to be the best we can become.

Mary Engelbreit

6

Picking Up the Tab

Dinner is over and you reach over to pick up the bill, secretly hoping someone else will reach for it too. They don't, and as usual you end up picking up the tab. What's so funny about that?

IS THAT ALL IT COSTS?

A lady in a faded gingham dress and her husband, dressed in a homespun, threadbare suit, stepped off the train in Boston, and walked timidly without an appointment into the Harvard University president's outer office. The secretary could tell in a moment that such backwoods, country hicks had no business at Harvard and probably didn't even deserve to be in Cambridge.

"We want to see the president," the man said softly. "He'll be busy all day," the secretary snapped. "We'll wait," the lady replied.

For hours the secretary ignored them, hoping that the couple would finally become discouraged and go away. They didn't and the secretary grew frustrated and finally decided to disturb the president, even though it was a chore she always regretted.

"Maybe if you see them for a few minutes, they'll leave," she said to him. He sighed in exasperation and nodded. Someone of his importance obviously didn't have the time to spend with them, but he detested gingham dresses and homespun suits cluttering up his outer office. The president, stern faced and with dignity, strutted toward the couple.

The lady told him, "We had a son who attended Harvard for one year. He loved Harvard. He was happy here. But about a year ago, he was accidentally killed. My husband and I would like to erect a memorial to him, somewhere on campus." The president wasn't touched. . . . He was shocked. "Madam," he said, gruffly, "we can't put up a statue for every person who attended Harvard and died. If we did, this place would look like a cemetery."

"Oh, no," the lady explained quickly. "We don't want to erect a statue. We thought we would like to give a building to Harvard." The president rolled his eyes. He glanced at the gingham dress and homespun suit, then exclaimed, "A building! Do you have any earthly idea how much a building costs? We have over seven and a half million dollars in the physical buildings here at Harvard."

For a moment the lady was silent. The president was pleased. Maybe he could get rid of them now.

"Is that all it costs to start a university? Why don't we just start our own?"

The lady turned to her husband and said quietly, "Is that all it costs to start a university? Why don't we just start our own?" Her husband nodded. The president's face wilted in confusion and bewilderment.

Mr. and Mrs. Leland Stanford got up and walked away, traveling to Palo Alto, California, where they established the university that bears their name, Stanford University, a memorial to a son that Harvard no longer cared about.

You can easily judge the character of others by how they treat those who they think can do nothing.

Malcolm Forbes

•••

If a parsley farmer goes bankrupt, can they garnish his wages?

Bruce Baum

Leigh, age 5, noted that the visitor next to her in the pew did not put money into the collection plate at her church in Atlanta.

"Hey, mister," she admonished, "you've got to PAY to go to this church."

Margaret Bigger

•••

You'll never guess what a tank of gas costs these days.

··

I'd rather be laughing on a bicycle than crying in a limousine.

Kathleen Russell

··

THE MONEY PIT

When money was tight, we considered buying an older car with only sixty thousand miles and a body that looked like new. Jacques, our mechanic from France, cautioned us: "Jou mus drive a car enough to keep zee rubber hoses and zee belts from cracking, Meeses St. John-Gilbair," he patiently explained. "Eef zee oil and lubrication 'ave not been changed regularly, zee engine, she may expire!" Jacques looked so foreboding, I almost lost my nerve.

But we needed a thriftier car. We reasoned that with all the money we would save on a new car payment, we would still be ahead, even if we made a few repairs. All we knew was we could afford it. So we sprang for it.

Before long, our mechanic-turned-prophet had his head permanently housed underneath the hood of our clunker. The hose sprang leaks like they'd had a run-in with Al Capone over a spaghetti dinner in Little Italy. At one point the driver's sideview mirror simply dropped off. Ditto with the rearview mirror. Soon we couldn't open the driver's door without first opening the back door. And the beat went on. But all of this paled compared to the catastrophic loss of the essential equipment that a person must have to survive the Amazon humidity of Virginia summers: air-conditioning.

Although the A/C was a goner, I was in denial. I turned obsessively optimistic as I flipped the switch on "high" every time I started the car. I guess I thought it might spontaneously leap to life one day. So with my hope alive and my A/C dead,

I urged my husband to let the mechanic search for the definitive answer to our sauna-mobile nightmares. A few months and twelve hundred dollars later, I was sitting yet again in the waiting area of Jacques's garage.

The agony of waiting for the A/C prognosis was more excruciating than waiting for my husband to come out of hernia surgery. Jacques emerged from under the hood of the car and stepped into the waiting area, gently settling beside me.

"We be friends long time, no?" he gingerly began.

"Yes, too long," I joked, trying to soften the blow I knew was coming. He did not smile.

"Dis car," he said, sadly shaking his head, "dis car no good. I no can fix the air."

I slumped and accepted the inevitable. Yes, the car had turned out to be a great deal—a great deal of trouble and expense. We eventually gave it to a minister friend and his wife. A few months later, our friends called to tell us the car had died. To which I said (no, screamed), "Good riddance!"

> Yes, the car had turned out to be a great deal— a great deal of trouble and expense.

Most of us, at one time or another, have possessions that turn into money pits. We shovel the dough in, hoping one more repair will do the trick. Too often we find ourselves singing "Nearer My God to Thee" while sinking on the ship of runaway costs.

Other things in life can be like that old clunker that we need to stop trying to revive and let die. The time may come with a project, possession, or even a relationship when we just need to let go. Perhaps God will resurrect it later or give us something better, but if we don't want to find ourselves in the poor house or the nut house, we might be better off to leave the decision to Him.

Rachel St. John Gilbert

CARNEGIE ENDOWMENT

Andrew Carnegie was a "limousine liberal" who firmly believed that the moneyed classes had a social responsibility, a view advocated in his book, *The Gospel of Wealth.*

Indeed, Carnegie provided funding for numerous social and educational projects (including many libraries), and was also a generous supporter of the New York Philharmonic Society.

One year the society's secretary visited Carnegie's mansion to request a $60,000 contribution. Carnegie, on the verge of signing a check, suddenly paused. "I've changed my mind," he declared. "Surely there are other people who like music enough to help with their own money." He then suggested that the secretary raise $30,000 from other donors, whereupon he would contribute the other half.

The following day the secretary returned to Carnegie's home to announce that he had already raised the requisite amount. Carnegie commended the man, wrote out his $30,000 check, and handed it over. "Would you mind telling me who gave you the other half?" he asked. "Not at all," the secretary replied. "Mrs. Carnegie."

Gene Fowler

• •

Some people pay their bills when due, some when overdue, and some never do.

Bob Phillips

• •

"Your stewardship sermons are improving.
Still no money, but a lot more IOUs."

IF IT'S BROKE, DON'T FIX IT

I have one basic approach to repair persons: I run as fast as I can in the opposite direction. It's the only way I know to avoid paying $200 to fix something worth $1.98. So on those rare occasions (roughly 150% of the time) when an appliance dies after its warranty has expired, I do what any rational individual would do: I consult *Consumer's Digest* and purchase a replacement.

I'll bet your ears perked up at the words *Consumer's Digest.* "She's one savvy buyer," you're telling yourself. Well, not exactly. All I really do is check the warranty lengths so I can schedule my next purchase. Let's say my new DVD player comes with a one-year guarantee. I simply mark "Day 366" on my calendar, and it breaks like clockwork.

I came by my Never Try to Fix It rule the hard way. I tried to repair a television set twice, at $75 a pop.

My first attempt seemed quite sensible. After all, the set was only five years old, and a new one would cost $400. Unfortunately it didn't seem quite so sensible when the TV self-destructed on the 91st day of my 90-day repair warranty.

But it was a good TV and hard to throw away, especially after a $75 investment. So I yelled a lot and, after getting no satisfaction, went out and found another repair person who was every bit the first fellow's equal.

Whoever said history repeats itself surely was thinking of me.

For years I've wondered why repairmen seldom effectively fix anything. And why their estimates incite so many bewildered customers to ditch the item and replace it.

The solution was simple: encourage fixers to either bungle the job, or to quote such ludicrous repair estimates that even a miser would opt to buy rather than repair.

After casting about for an answer, I finally coaxed it out of my favorite government inside, whom I can identify only as "Deep Wrench." He clued me in to a little-known law passed in 1959—right before things started to fall apart. Known as the "Make Them Buy Stuff Act," or MTBS, it was modeled on the federal subsidy for farmers. We pay farmers not to farm. Why pay fixers not to fix? So argued the lobbyists representing appliance manufacturers all over America.

In the '50s, skillful repairmen were so good at their jobs and so reasonably priced that a manufacturer couldn't even make a sale to his mother. After all, why purchase a replacement when someone was willing and able to fix your appliance without demanding to be named in your will?

The solution was simple: encourage fixers to either bungle the job, or to quote such ludicrous repair estimates that even a miser would opt to buy rather than repair.

How do you accomplish this? Easily. Just pay repairmen a healthy percentage of the profits on replacement appliances. The idea was swiftly adopted and, unlike our appliances, the scheme functions flawlessly.

Now that Deep Wrench has unraveled the repair person puzzle, it's time for me to tackle some other pressing national predicament. And I'll gladly do it, as soon as someone volunteers to pay me not to write.

Madeleine Begun Kane

●●

H. L. Hunt, one of the wealthiest people in the world, explained why he gave up cigars: "It was costing $300,000 per year of my time to unwrap them!"

Joe Taylor Ford

●●

MISQUOTED

While on vacation in Dublin, Ireland, Henry Ford visited an orphanage where a building project was being planned. The director of the fund-raising committee decided to make a call on the famous and rich man, Henry Ford. After their discussion Ford judged the cause a worthy one, and so he wrote out a check then and there for 2,000 pounds, which was quite a gift.

His generosity was so incredible it made the headlines of the local newspaper. The problem was, they misquoted the figure and reported, "Ford gave 20,000 pounds."

The director of the orphanage called Henry Ford to apologize. In fact, he said, "I'll be happy to phone the editor right away and correct the mistake."

But, feeling a little guilty, Ford said that there was no need for that. With a sigh, he took out his pen and checkbook and said, "I'll give you a check for the remaining 18,000 pounds." But he made only one request. He said, "When the new building opens, I want this inscription put on it, 'I was a stranger and you took me in.'"

Clifton Fadiman

•••

The have and have nots can often be traced back to the did and did nots.

D. O. Flynn

•••

"Of course I'm afraid to have kids! My initials are A.T.M."

....

Where I was brought up we never talked about money because there was never enough to furnish a topic of conversation.

Mark Twain

....

GO AHEAD—SHARE YOUR BASKET

Though a touch of winter chill was in the air, the Easter morning held a promise of warmth that would come with the rising sun.

Across the room Raylinda Dupree, the scourge of my childhood, slept soundly. My cousin twice-removed on my mama's side, Raylinda was the meanest person I knew. In fact, she was the meanest person most people knew. She lived with us after her parents divorced and quickly made an impression on the other residents of Posey Road. Within days of her arrival she had been awarded various nicknames including, but not limited to, "Satan's Star Student." While I know God loves us all, Raylinda certainly did put her best efforts into earning her reputation.

Snoring loudly, Raylinda stirred only when Mama mentioned two words—*Easter baskets!* Racing to the dining room table, Raylinda and I found two wicker baskets crammed with all the items essential to the Posey Road Easter Basket. Atop green plastic grass sat colorful luscious eggs, tangy jellybeans, tiny football-shaped chocolate wrapped in pastel foil, yellow marshmallow chicks, and a vast collection of speckled malted milk eggs. Four wrapped eggs with various fruit fillings were placed strategically at north, south, east, and west within the basket. A hollow bunny inside a colorful box rested amid the green grass. And, of course, the traditional focal point of the basket was a large coconut egg covered in chocolate with a candy flower adorning the top.

As I examined my basket, I realized that Raylinda had

disappeared. While I considered her absence an Easter blessing, Mama was frustrated. It was going to be a busy day
beginning with the annual Sunrise Service at 6:30 A.M.
Because Mama played the piano, we could not be late for
church. Breakfast and Sunday school would follow the Sunrise
Service. At 11:00 A.M. our little church would fill with people
dressed in their Easter best, many of whom we had not seen
since Christmas. People would happily greet one another and
a festive spirit would fill the air. We would sing my favorite
Easter hymn, *"Up from the grave He arose with a mighty triumph
o'er his foes"* with a force that shook the walls in celebration.

Raylinda, of course, sang her own version: *"Up from the
grave He arose with a trumpet sticking in His nose."* She sang
loudly and off-key while many stared and frowned
at "Satan's Star Student."

After church, we hurried home and waited for
extended friends and family to arrive for a huge
Easter dinner. Mama baked ham and everyone
brought food to share. The general idea was to eat
until you could barely move.

There was an unspoken rule that the ladies
would each try to outdo each other when it came
to dessert. There was a 5-layer strawberry cake
with fresh strawberries decorating the top. An
Italian cream cake was Aunt Zelma's annual contribution. There was always a huge banana pud-
ding (Oh Lord, I hate bananas!). Then, of course,
there were several new recipes straight from the
pages of the latest *Good Housekeeping* or *Southern Living* magazines. While some adults did indulge in these exquisite
homemade offerings, many simply wanted a couple of
malted eggs to top off their ham and potato salad. Those decisions, of course, only irritated the bakers of the *Good
Housekeeping* and *Southern Living* fancy desserts.

> There was
> an unspoken
> rule that the
> ladies would
> each try to
> outdo each
> other when
> it came to
> dessert.

This was the moment each child brought his or her Easter basket to show and share. The only object not subject to sharing, said Mama, was our large coconut egg. It was safely tucked away in the back of the refrigerator. Everything else was fair game and communal property. In other words, it was open season on Easter baskets.

About this time I finally understood the reason for Raylinda's strange disappearance earlier that morning. As she begrudgingly shared her basket, it swiftly passed from one person to the next. No one partook of any item in Raylinda's basket. When I looked closely, I instantly discovered the reason. It was clearly evident that someone had taken a bite out of every piece of candy in the basket. Each tiny egg had been unwrapped and nibbled. Teeth marks adorned every jellybean and malted milk piece. The hollow chocolate bunny rattled inside his box because someone had chewed away his ears. And every innocent little marshmallow chick was headless!

Adults were appalled. Other kids were angry. Granny gasped and held her chest. Aunt Zelma became woozy with the vapors.

The basket was a sacrilege. Blasphemy on Easter Sunday! Who would perform such a cruel, selfish act?

The answer was obvious to me. To keep from sharing, Satan's Star Student had taken a bite out of every object in her basket. She was stingy. She was mean. And she had just demonstrated that truth to everyone present.

Her shameful behavior never changed. Not only did Raylinda succeed in protecting her basket that particular Easter, she continued to do so each year. No one wanted to partake of the damaged goods in her basket so she succeeded in keeping all candy to herself. Raylinda easily kept her well-earned reputation of being the meanest, greediest person I knew.

Raylinda's greed did not stop Easter, of course. It simply

proved that all humans are flawed in one way or another—some perhaps more than others! Years later, I realize that Raylinda, in her selfishness, demonstrated one of the real truths of the season.

Easter is not about greed. It has nothing to do with selfishness.

Easter has everything to do with love and sharing. It celebrates a wondrous moment when, to a flawed world, God gave His very best in the form of a child in a manger. God gave this gift to each of us, fully and freely, holding nothing back.

No, Easter is not about greed. Therefore, we should never hesitate to share the Good News of Easter with everyone.

There are many things I will never understand. But this I do know—God gave His best to us. And God expects the best from us.

So, I suppose, it is possible to learn a positive lesson even from Raylinda Dupree, the scourge of my childhood and "Satan's Star Student." Thank God for the blessing of Jesus Christ and the priceless gift of eternal life. Then, in a spirit of true gratitude, praise God by joyfully and unselfishly sharing your basket!

Cathy Lee Phillips

· ·

There is one advantage of being poor—a doctor will cure you faster.

Kin Hubbard

Money—if you'll excuse the expression—is like manure. It's not worth anything unless it is spread around to make things grow!

Hello, Dolly!

· ·

"Have you been paying through the nose for your prescriptions? I found a twenty dollar bill lodged in your sinuses."

MORE THAN WILLING

Rick and Elaine have embraced a genuine transfer of wills—they have surrendered their own will and joyfully submitted to the will of Christ for their lives. Rick has been a phenomenally successful businessman, and God has blessed them with substantial financial resources. Not long ago, Rick approached me before Christmas and said, "God has been so good to us. Elaine and I don't want to do anything for each other, but together we want to give and help some families in need."

Our church was involved in a number of community outreach efforts, but Rick and Elaine wanted to do something on a personal level. I'm ashamed to admit it, but in my own busyness and distraction during the Christmas season, I failed to follow up with them. Needless to say, I felt terrible when I encountered Rick in the weeks after Christmas.

Rick was gracious. He assured me that my inaction did not

stop their generous impulse. But he went on to say, "I want you to know, I really want to help with people you meet who have a need. There will be a future opportunity. And when you hear of it, be sure to give me a call."

As the new year started to roll, weeks turned into months. But then came a second chance.

While making a hospital visit, I received a message to return the call of a woman whose name I did not initially recognize. As we spoke, she said that her daughter and mine were friends. She went on to explain that she was a single parent. And she related her daughter's desperate desire to change schools.

Her daughter was a freshman at a local high school, and she told her mom that the atmosphere and conditions of her school were making her miserable. She begged her mother to submit an application to attend a Christian school associated with our church. Then the mother leveled with me: "I told her there was no way we could ever afford for her to attend a private school."

After months of resistance, this single mother took a simple step of faith. She filled out an application to the Christian school. She could afford the application fee, so she submitted a request for admission and financial aid. Before long, the response came from the school that her daughter was accepted. The school was able to offer her some financial aid, but the remaining balance was greater than this mother's diligent work and sacrifice could absorb.

Having come so far but still being so far away, she called me to see if I knew of any options. I listened. I sensed the passion and pain in the voice of this mother, who desperately wanted to provide something more for her daughter but didn't know where to turn or how to get it. After she shared, we prayed. I told her that I did not have any ability to tap additional resources but that I would continue to pray.

After we finished talking, I thought about Rick and Elaine.

I was uncertain as to whether I should make a call. Private education was not exactly the type of "family need" I understood them to want to provide. However, I decided to let them make the decision and placed the call.

When we spoke later that evening, Rick was planning to leave the country for a business trip to East Asia. Though he was busy getting ready for the trip, he asked me to tell him about the girl and the tuition. And then he said this: "I want you to call this mother back and tell her that we are thrilled to be able to make up the difference for her daughter to make the move to a Christian school this year. And there is something else. We want you to tell her that we will provide the balance of this need until she graduates!"

Tears filled my eyes as I heard these words. This was so much more than she or I could have imagined.

> But she could never have imagined how that simple step of faith could be met with God's overwhelming supply.

Here was a single mother, working hard and sacrificing to do all she could to support and provide for her daughter. She did what she could do, submitted an application, and paid an admission fee. But she could never have imagined how that simple step of faith could be met with God's overwhelming supply.

It wasn't a *money* thing; it was a *will* thing. Rick and Elaine had made a transfer in their hearts, and they were willing to do the will of God. And they wanted to do it in a way that would truly impact the life of another.

A single mother sought God's will for her daughter. A high school student wanted God's will for her future. A couple desired to do God's will with their resources. And as the pastor in the middle, I shared money I didn't have with a mother I didn't know and saw a young woman experience an opportunity I couldn't give and a joy I can't fully describe all from people pursuing the will of God. His will is good, acceptable, and perfect. No wonder the psalmist declared, "Oh, taste and see that the LORD is good; blessed is the man who trusts in Him!" (Psalm 34:8).

David McKinley

7

The Infernal Revenue Service

The IRS has become an acronym that strikes fear and frustration in our hearts. It's also become the target of our jokes and pokes when it comes to our financial focus.

MORE INFORMATION, PLEASE

Dear IRS:

I have received your letter regarding my 1040 federal individual income tax return. When I went to the mailbox, it was right there among all the bills in a plain white envelope—plain except for three little words in the return address "Internal Revenue Service."

I thought that perhaps you were writing to thank me for my contribution to the national budget and to wish me a large, taxable income this year. But you simply said you had received my tax return and that you needed more information to process it accurately.

Now I know that I accidentally underpaid a few years ago, but I didn't think you would continue to hold a grudge. Last time it was three years before you caught the error. I would like to congratulate you on your improvement in promptness.

I noticed that you said to enclose only the information requested; however, you had not yet requested anything. You also said, "Do not send a copy of your return." Why would I do that when you already have said that you have received my Form 1040? So far compliance is not an issue.

> **You really do need to do something about your pessimism.**

What really upset me was when you said that if you do not hear from me within 20 days that you may have to increase the tax I owe or reduce my refund. You really do need to do something about your pessimism.

Finally, you got around to the real purpose of the letter: "Your Form 1040 doesn't show your original signature. Please sign the declaration below."

So, I forgot to sign my tax return? That's it? No fine? No penalty? No audit? Not that I'm disappointed or anything, mind you.

I really couldn't figure out the rest of the letter. You said:

"If this is a join return, both husband and wife must sign." But you already said that you have received my return. Didn't you look at it to see whose name was on it?

"If you can't write your name, please sign your mark." Well, I'll admit that there are a lot of people who think I can't write, but I don't believe they are referring to my name.

"If you are signing as a parent of the minor child, sign both the child's name and your name." Thanks, but we established in number one that you received my return, and that you obviously didn't bother to look at the name on it.

"A power of attorney is needed in all other instances." There you go, flaunting your clout again. You must stay up nights programming computers to write intimidating letters.

So, all you really want is for me to sign my name on the affidavit and return it? I don't know why you had to get so huffy about it. I signed the check I sent you, didn't I?

Thanks, however, for offering to answer my questions. I don't have any questions, but I thought I'd write anyhow just to show that there are no hard feelings. Actually, I believe I said what you wanted to hear in April—even if I didn't sign it.

It was also nice of you to apologize for any inconvenience, especially, since I'm the one that apparently inconvenienced you. You may rest assured that I won't make that mistake again.

Also, I would like to call to your attention the fact that the signature on your letter does NOT appear to be ORIGINAL. Therefore, I've enclosed an affidavit for you to sign. Please return it within 20 days.

Thanks and have a great year!

Sincerely yours,
A Taxpayer

Sheila Moss

• •

Money really isn't everything. If it was, what would we buy with it?

Tom Wilson

• •

THE ROLLING PIN

Every family has something that is passed down through the generations. In ours, it's a glass rolling pin that dates back to the Great Depression. It's shaped like a bottle, designed to be filled with hot water. It was given to my mother by my grandma. "Here's another way to make it valuable," my mother said, plunking in a penny she'd found on the sidewalk. She started adding spare change, saving for a rainy day. That day came when a neighbor, Lorraine, stopped by for tea. "Please pray for my family," Lorraine said. Her husband was offered a job out of town. He didn't have money for gas to get him through the week.

"But I do!" Mother said. She emptied the change onto Lorraine's lap. Mother kept filling the rolling pin. Each time it was full, she would hear of someone in need and give it to them.

Just before her eightieth birthday, she gave the rolling pin to me. "Now it's your turn."

Emma Glover

"Opportunity? Opportunity Who?"

. . . .

Blessed are the young, for they shall inherit the national debt.

Herbert Hoover

A man explained why he bought his new car. "I was faced with the choice of buying a $32 battery for my old car or an $8,000 car—and they wanted cash for the battery."

Author Unknown

. . . .

YOU CAN BANK ON IT

Do you have a hard time saving money? You fully intended to deposit some of your babysitting cash into your savings account, but on the way to the bank you drove by Foot Locker and just had to stop for a new pair of hightops. After that you found yourself in the drive-through at Burger King, which, oddly enough, funneled you right into the parking lot of Macy's department store where they were having a huge summer fashion clearance.

By the time you got to the bank, you had 56 cents left. Add that to the $1.18 that was already in your account, and that swells your life savings to a grand total of $1.74!

It's hard to save. It's difficult to put away for the future when we're living in the *now*.

There is one bank account, however, where you can quickly accumulate wealth. It's the First Bank of Good Deeds and Faithful Service to the Lord. This bank doesn't close at 3:00 p.m. You can make deposits twenty-four hours a day, seven days a week, and each deposit is posted immediately.

This bank pays the highest interest around, too. Each deposi-
tor gets a mansion to live in, mortgage free, for all eternity.
That sure beats three, four, or even ten percent.

Don't get me wrong. It's a good idea to be wise with our
money here on earth, to save as much as we can. But the
deposits that really count are the ones we make with God.

Martha Bolton

· ·

**Said of money: I don't necessarily like it, but it
quiets my nerves.**

Joe Louis

**The IRS sent back my tax return saying I owed
eight hundred dollars. I said, "If you'll notice, I
sent a paper clip with my return. Given what
you've been paying for things lately, that should
more than make up the difference."**

Emo Philips

· ·

SINGIN' THE TAX SEASON BLUES

It's that time again. Time to set up the folding card table in
the living room, sharpen the pencils, gather the 1099s, con-
sume a few pots of coffee, and dive into the process we all
know and don't love. Filing your taxes!

Americans have come to accept this process as a right of
passage for living in this great country, but for some of us, it's
still a pretty overwhelming and intimidating event. In fact, I

really don't know anyone who looks forward to this annual occasion except maybe accountants and the IRS. Both make a pretty penny from the whole ordeal and I bet some individuals even get downright giddy about all of the number crunching.

> Not me! I'd rather be crunching a bag of chips or simply watching paint dry.

Not me! I'd rather be crunching a bag of chips or simply watching paint dry. No matter how many years I've gone through this process, every time it's the same thing. Dread. Dismay. Despair. And downloading data until I'm blue in the face. And here's a question for you. Anybody else wondering why the popular program people use to do their taxes is called Quicken? Personally, I didn't find it to be too quick. But then again, perhaps that's because I hadn't downloaded any data since 12/31/04. And let me tell you, what a difference a year makes! When I started downloading my 2005 data it was January and there was a blanket of snow covering the ground. By the time I finished, it was March and the daffodils were popping up like H&R Block offices during this time of year.

I really don't know how I became the "chosen one" for this miserable task. It's definitely not because I'm the financial whiz of this marriage. I mean, c'mon. I'm a writer and everybody knows that creative people use the non-tax filing side of their brain for their creativity. This is also clearly the reason I switched my major in college from accounting to communications after my third semester. I mean, what was I thinking?

What's even more ironic is the fact that my husband works for a software company that generates 1099s and other tax forms for brokerage firms and banks, so it's obvious who wears the financial pants in this family. But here's the thing. Because of my husband's job, during the height of tax season he is in such high demand making sure all of these forms are produced without a glitch that he is literally putting in 80–100 hours weeks. Obviously, it's not his favorite time of the year either. So, what does that mean? It means he's exhausted and I get the honor of doing our taxes.

I guess that's OK. I suppose I can "take one for the team." After all, I did promise "for better or for worse." So what's a floundering financial housewife supposed to do? Pass the buck! Since I strongly believe you should let the professionals do what they do best, it makes sense to let an accountant file our taxes. Sure, an accountant costs more than the latest version of Turbo Tax, but in my mind, it's worth every penny. I mean, one person's write-off could be another person's red flag to the IRS screaming, "Please audit me." And with my luck, if I filed our taxes the IRS would be banging on my door waving a sea of red flags prepared to perform the nation's longest audit ever. No, thanks. I'll gladly hand over the reins to my trusty CPA.

The good news . . . we're getting a refund back from Uncle Sam. The bad news . . . well, Ben Franklin said it best. "In this world the only thing that is certain is death and taxes."

Hmmmmmm. Suddenly, I love taxes!

Kathryn S. Mahoney

• •

Beware of little expenses: a small leak will sink a great ship.

Benjamin Franklin

"I think you're a nice kid. I've known you for about five years. Could you let me have five dollars?"

"I'm sorry—I couldn't."

"Why?"

"Because I have known *you* for five years."

Bob Phillips

• •

You can't take it with you ... but you CAN
send it on ahead.

A kid swallowed a coin and it got stuck in his throat. His mother yelled for help. A man passing by hit him in the small of the back and the coin came out.

"I don't know how to thank you, Doctor . . .," his mother started.

"I'm not a doctor," the man replied. "I'm from the IRS."

Brian Becker

••

Government said Americans are all geographically illiterate and economically ignorant. It's true. How many times have you said to yourself: "Where did all my money go?"

Alan Prophet

••

HELP YOURSELF TO THE COLLECTION PLATE!

In this age of massive finance, with its grand-scale advertising campaigns and giant public relations agencies, the church is frequently caught between the very real economic needs of its projects, and high pressure methods of fund-raising.

Yet if the world has changed, the message of the gospel has not; those simple, direct truths of life and human nature have, if anything, greater significance today than ever before.

Recently, during one Sabbath day service, Pastor Carl Raphael of the Seventh Day Adventist Church outside Sydney, Australia, recalled from his pulpit the Parable of the Talents for his congregation of 150 men, women, and children. Ushers then walked the aisles carrying a collection plate piled high with $140 in one and two dollar notes.

Pastor Raphael told his people to take as much as they liked. He asked only that they use the money as did the "good and faithful servants" of Christ's Parable of the Talents, and that they make it grow.

The "good servants," you remember, were the ones who took the "talents" their Lord had given them and, by ingenuity, increased the value of these a hundredfold, in expectation of the reckoning the master would make on his return.

What happened in Pastor Raphael's small, but dedicated, congregation might well become a pattern for giving in our own country.

Robyn and Edwin Whatson of Sydney turned their few dollars into $106. "I bought honey in 60-pound jars for seven dollars," Mrs. Whatson recalls, "poured it into smaller jars I scrounged from friends, and sold it for 40 cents a pound." After five months there was $40.

For his part Mr. Whatson bought and resold shirts and rugs at a profit of $66. Having gotten the items at a low price himself, he was able to sell them for only slightly more, and still offer a bit of a bargain.

Mrs. Winifred Burnett "speculated" in guinea pigs. She and her family bred them full pelt at their home. As fast as the new piglets came along they were sold, either to people as pets, or to Sydney University as—guinea pigs.

Mrs. Su Fong, from Hong Kong, took one dollar. With it she bought the ingredients for fried rice, made it and then sold it for a profit. With her increased money she purchased packets of soup, added water, boiled the mixture and sold that—also for a small profit. It was enough to make her dollar keep on growing. Then she donned her Saturday-best, a burgundy-colored woolen dress with matching hat, walked with her husband the half mile from her home to the church and handed the pastor $20.

Aleaphea Parr wanted to do something special. Mrs. Parr brought certain bottles into the house that had never before been anywhere on the teetotaling Parrs' premises. Square-shaped whiskey bottles, curvaceous Chianti bottles, elegant Benedictine bottles—each of them different.

Then she went out and compared prices of small mosaic tiles and found the best buy to be a line that sells for 80 cents a square foot. These tiles she glued permanently to the outside of the bottles. While a friend drilled a hole in the base of the bottles and fitted them with lightbulbs, Mrs. Parr got to work making lampshades out of fiberglass and linen. Each completed lamp averaged about $5.50 to make. She sold them for about $8 apiece. Mrs. Parr's profit for the pastor was $60.50.

Results from the original $140 increased to over $500.

And so it went throughout the congregation, including the pastor himself. Results from the original $140 increased to over $500; as in the Parable of the Talents the crisis was more than met. But besides the immediate practical effects of the project there was a much greater lesson to be learned from this modern-day example of stewardship; these were the beginnings of the fulfillment of a promise. "Well done, thou good and faithful servant: thou hast been faithful over a few things, I will make thee ruler over many things: enter into the joy of thy lord" (KJV Matt 25:21).

Adapted from Daily Telegraph, *Sydney, Australia*

"You want an extension? Sure — I'll take my break and be back in fifteen minutes."

I'm living so far beyond my income that we may almost be said to be living apart.

e. e. cummings

•••

The minister was ignorant of financial matters. He once received a check—the first one he ever saw in his life—and took it to a bank for payment. "You must first endorse the check," said the teller, returning it through the little window. "It must be endorsed on the back."

"I see," said the minister. And turning the check over he wrote across the back of it, "I heartily endorse this check."

Ken Alley

•••

LESS IS MORE

A church board decided that people in the congregation were embarrassed when the offering plates were passed. So they thought they ought to have a new system that wouldn't embarrass anybody, especially those who couldn't give. They asked the pastor to design a way of handling it so people could give as they came in or went out. So he built several interesting boxes and put them at each door. But these boxes were different. If you dropped in a dollar or more, it made no noise, it was silent. If you gave a half dollar, a little bell tingled. If you gave a quarter, it blew a whistle. If you gave a dime, a siren went off. If you gave a nickel, a shot sounded. If you gave nothing, it took your picture!

Clyde Murdock

TAKE THE MONEY AND . . .

From the Internal Revenue Service Publication 525, page 13, category Miscellaneous Taxable Income, subcategory Illegal Income: "Illegal income, such as stolen or embezzled funds, must be included in your gross income on line 21 of Form 1040, or on Schedule C-EZ if from your self-employment activity."

Mary Ann Andera

COUGH IT UP!

Drug dealers, muggers, and thieves are expected to cough up their taxes just like the rest of us—and they're also allowed to deduct business expenses. These are legitimate criminal deductions:

Hit man: Bullets, mileage for driving to target
Counterfeiter: Printing press, green ink, paper
Moonshiner: Corn, wire coils for still
Arsonist: Matches, rags
Cattle rustler: Rope.

Jenny McCune

• •

Actual call to the IRS: Hi, I'm a bookkeeper, and I need to know if ten $100 bills make $1,000 or only ten hundred dollars.

IRS: Both, it's the same amount.

Caller: So why do I get a different answer every time I move the decimal point?

Jim Kraus

• •

LIFE AS AN IRS AGENT

To hear him tell it, Mr. Roderick Jacquesnif-Flemface (whose last name, according to him, is pronounced: Flahm-fah-Say), is an average, hardworking conscientious person just like you or me. Mr. Flemface, in point of fact, works for the Internal Revenue Service. He claimed to this interviewer that being thus employed causes him to be abused by people he meets socially, abandoned in restaurants by the few dates he manages to get, and accounts for the fact that he is still unmarried at age 52.

Mr. Flemface told me that he sought counsel from other IRS co-workers on how they managed to fool someone into marrying them. They advised him to follow their lead and deny any involvement with the infamous government agency until after he was safely hitched.

"Why do that?" I asked a certain Mr. Ivor Yurnstayne, a fellow employee who insisted that I not name him, under penalty of consequences he preferred I not divulge.

"Well," well'ed Mr. Yurnstayne, "decent people don't want to have anything to do with us, so in order to latch onto a spouse, we have to resort to either marrying one another, or else use deception, deceit, dishonesty, and other tactics adopted from the workplace."

"Is it as bad as all that?" I asked Mr. Flemface.

"The only ones who have it worse than us finding someone who is willing to share bed, board, and saliva, are Meter Maids."

"Really?" I replied.

"Well, knowing what they do for a living, would you marry a Meter Maid?"

Of course, I saw his point at once. There are some things that decent, morally sensitive folk should not be expected to do.

Mr. Flemface continued relating his harrowing experiences to me. He asked me to imagine his dismay when, standing at the altar and exchanging vows with his Lovely Intended, he heard her say, "I do . . . unless, of course, he works for the IRS!"

But even more painful was what happened at the instantly canceled wedding immediately after the revelation of who his employer really was: Mr. Flemface was gang-slapped by the bride's family, kick-stomped by the six-year-old Ring Bearer, and rose-whipped by the Flower Girl.

Still, it was the closest he'd ever been to marriage and he savors the memory of it.

> It's prejudice! Why should I be treated shabbily just because I work for the IRS?

"It's discrimination!" exclaims Mr. Flemface to anyone who will listen. (Which is hardly anyone.) "It's prejudice! Why should I be treated shabbily just because I work for the IRS?"

I suggested that if it caused him such anguish, perhaps he ought to quit the IRS and seek other employment.

Mr. Flemface retorted: "Why should I? Where else could I find a job that allows me to pry into people's personal lives, strike such soul-satisfying fear and discomfort into their hearts, bully and harass them, discourage and intimidate the small business persons, take huge gobbles out of their hard-earned money, force people to spend their own money and man-hours doing my bookkeeping to figure out how much money they owe me, while I gleefully and constantly change the rules, perks, and percentages in mid-stream at my every whim like an oriental potentate?"

"Well I . . ." I began, though he did not seem to notice.

"And then I get to take what the people pay me and turn it over to other government agencies who will wantonly waste it with an irresponsible profligacy that would be criminal in a private business. Plus, I have my own court system so I'm free to define justice as I see fit rather than have to submit to some dreary old constitution that says I shouldn't exist anyway."

"Well I . . ." I began again with not much hope of getting to continue. And I wasn't disappointed.

"Plus, why should I miss out on the means to inflate my sense of power and self-importance at the expense of others and on top of it all get paid for it with a commission for every ounce of blood I squeeze out of these turnips?!"

"Point taken," I answered. And before I could stop myself, after the briefest of pauses, I added: "Flemface . . ."

"That's Mister Flemface, to you."

"Okay, Mister Flemface," I spat back.

"Tut, tut, tut," Mr. Flemface tutted. "Can you say audit?"

"Hmm . . ."

Gene-Michael Higney

THANKS ANYWAY!

A little boy needed $100 for a school field trip, so his mother told him to ask God for it. He prayed for two weeks, but nothing turned up. So he decided to ask God for the money in a letter.

At the post office, the postmaster opened the letter to God and decided to forward it to the President of the United States.

The President was charmed, so he told his secretary to send the boy $5. After receiving the money, the boy wrote a thank-you letter to God.

"Dear God, Thank you very much for sending the money. I noticed that you had to send it through Washington. As usual, those guys deducted $95. Thanks anyway!"

Jim Kraus

CHURCH OF THE COVERED DISH by Thom Tapp

A TAXING SITUATION

When I looked at my calendar, a huge red circle around Friday slapped me in the face. Today was Wednesday. I only had two days left to come up with $22,343.70 to pay the IRS, and I had no clue from where that much money could possibly come. My heart was pounding like Thumper the rabbit, sending ominous vibrations to my stressed-out brain. What was I going to do?

I'd already run out of extensions. I'd filed one in April and the second one in August (doesn't everyone?), because I didn't have the money to pay my tax bill. So the jig was up and I had to face the music. It was do-or-die time, and I could imagine Uncle Sam's finger pointing at me saying, "I want you!"

I had a couple of royalty payments that I'd been trying to collect for months, but those were certainly not forthcoming. Still, I decided to make the call out of sheer desperation.

"Hey, Jerry, this is Mary." And I related to him my dilemma. "Any chance you've received the royalty checks we've been waiting for? I've run out of other options, and I could surely use your help."

"I don't think so, Mary, but I'll check and call you back."

"Okay, Jere. Thanks."

For the next three hours I racked my brain trying to figure out what to do, looking for any kind of resource, praying for help from above. I drummed my fingers, tapped my foot, paced around my office, and generally drove myself crazy thinking of what might happen next. When the phone rang at 4:30, I nearly jumped out of my skin.

"Hello!" I almost yelled.

"Mary, this is Jerry. Well, I think I have a little good news for you. As it turns out, we did receive one of the checks we've been waiting for. It came in yesterday's mail. My accountant just hadn't mentioned it to me."

"Wonderful!" I yelped. "Could you tell me how much my part is and how soon you can get it to me?"

"Yes, your portion is $13,700, and I can overnight it to you today."

"Jerry, have I told you lately that I love you?" I laughed. "You're a life saver!"

"I'll get it into FedEx right now, Mary. And I'm glad I could help, at least a little."

"Me too! And thanks so much, Jerry."

"Wahoo! Wahoo!" I chirped as I danced around my office. *At least I can send the IRS a token of my esteem and pray they'll be lenient about the rest*, I thought. *IRS . . . lenient . . . fat chance!*

I sat down at my desk and began to fill out the paperwork to submit the partial payment I would be able to make. But my mind was still in turmoil, trying to figure out where I could scrape up another $8,643.70. Do the words "bottom of the barrel" convey what I was feeling?

Needless to say, I slept very little that night, tossing and turning, looking into the inky night, trying to keep my blood pressure under control. And I arose Thursday morning with bleary eyes and cobwebs in my brain from lack of rest. I stumbled to the kitchen and made a pot of strong coffee, knowing I'd probably need it to get through this worrisome day, and poured myself a cup of the black sunshine.

I spent the morning staying as busy as I could to distract myself from the depressing thoughts of being up to my ears in debt to the IRS with little or no prospect of solving the problem.

When FedEx delivered the express letter from Jerry, I took the check directly to the bank to deposit, grabbed a quick hot dog at the Sonic and came back home. I wrote my check for the full $13,700 and started to put it in the IRS envelope when the phone rang.

"Hey, Mary, this is Jerry."

"Hi, Jere. Listen, thanks so much for sending the check. It arrived safely, and I've deposited it. So I can at least pay part of my taxes."

"Well, don't mail that check yet," he said. "Guess what came in my mail today?"

My heart stopped. "No, don't tell me," I said quietly.

"Yes, the other long-awaited royalty check. Can you believe it?" he laughed.

I couldn't even respond. I was so dumbfounded, I was in complete shock.

Jerry went on. "I'll overnight this one to you today so you'll have it in the morning."

"Thanks, Jerry. You can't know what an incredible relief this is. How much is my part of this one?"

I was holding my breath. Would it actually be enough to cover the remaining taxes?

"Your part is $8,650."

It took a few second for me to do the mental calculation,

and then it registered—God had sent me $6.30 too much! I started to laugh, jump up and down, and dance around the room. I was astounded . . . flabbergasted . . . and so humbled by the realization that God's timing, as usual, was absolutely perfect. "Ask and you will receive" suddenly took on infinitely more meaning to me.

That night, as you can imagine, I slept like a baby. My blood pressure returned to normal, and my prayers were said with joy.

The second check arrived by FedEx the next morning. So I wrote my check to the IRS and put it in the envelope, which had to be postmarked that day. I went by the bank and made the deposit, then dropped the letter off at the post office with a huge sigh of relief.

> **I went by the bank and made the deposit, then dropped the letter off at the post office with a huge sigh of relief.**

Then to celebrate, I drove to Chili's restaurant for lunch. I ordered a cheeseburger, fries, and iced tea. As I ate my lunch, I once again thanked God for his grace and generosity. I was still overwhelmed by what had happened.

When I finished my meal, I wiped my hands on my napkin, took out my wallet, and turned over the check. Tears began to roll down my face when I saw that the bill, including the needed tip, came to exactly $6.30.

Mary Hollingsworth

Americans seem to believe that we have the right to life, love, and the *purchase* of happiness.

Rick Atchley

AS THE OLD YEAR FADES, SO DOES MY MEMORY

Memory is a very tricky thing, at least for me it is. Looking back, over a year's span of activity my memory seems to pick and choose what it remembers. It amazes me not so much what a person remembers but what a person forgets.

Often some old-timer will moan about how much he missed the good old days. I'm not sure if he is thinking of World War II or the Great Depression. I'm positive that during the Great Depression some wonderful memories were created, but I'm not sure anyone wants to return to those thrilling days of yesterday.

The bad was not as bad as we remember and the good was not as good as we boast.

Some things are best forgotten and some things should never be forgotten; my trouble has always been remembering which is which. (Personally, I don't know the difference between "which" and "that").

Several things about the old year bear serious consideration. The past year, in my opinion was not just one year but several years flowing together. Sometimes I'm not sure which year I lived.

The year 2004, like all its brothers before it, actually consisted of three years.

First, there is the year that really was. "Just the facts, ma'am."

I'm a little fuzzy about this one. For one thing, looking at my checkbook entries (at least the ones I remembered to enter) the past year was a completely different one than I recall.

I really do not recollect having all the fun indicated by my bank statement. Why is it that no matter how much money I put into my bank account, more money comes out?

Evidently, some phantom creature has access to my checkbook.

President Ronald Reagan was accused of voodoo economics. Reviewing my bank statements, I could be accused of "Who-do" economics.

My income tax statement is another perplexity. I can never figure it out. If the government said I made that much money, I must have made that much money and owe that much in taxes.

Speaking of the government, what I don't understand is how they know how much I owe, to the penny, along with millions of other Americans and cannot find Osama bin Laden. I know exactly how to solve this conundrum.

One surefire way of finding him is leaking to the government that Osama bin Laden owes taxes and he will be caught before April 15, guaranteed.

James L. Snyder

OUR BIG-TICKET ITEM

The annual garage sale is a tradition in our family; it's a chance to get rid of old clothes, used toys, old kitchen utensils. Usually I can count on the profits from the sale to pay for a few extras on our family vacation, and this year we had one item that would be sure to bring in good money: our youngest daughter's bedroom suite. As I inspected the pink bedspreads, the white polished dresser, the sturdy bunk beds, I could almost feel the money in my pocket.

Customers began lining up before breakfast. At 8:45 I gave the tables a final dusting and we let the people in. A woman with a newborn sorted through the baby clothes; a well-dressed gentleman bought all of Bob's outdated ties. And soon not just one, but two women were interested in the bedroom suite.

"Would you come down on your price?" one of them asked.

"No," I replied. "Two hundred dollars seems fair."

"Well, here," she said. "Take my number. My name is Stevens. If you don't get what you want for it by the end of the day, give me a call."

I placed her number in the cash box and closed the lid, dreaming of our vacation. Maybe we could go white water rafting with the extra money. Or perhaps Bob and I could afford new hiking boots.

Later in the morning I came out to find Bob talking to a young couple near the furniture. The woman was pregnant and holding the hands of twin four-year-old girls. The young man had one arm in a cast; with the other he was holding the hand of a seven-year-old boy. *Perfect customers for our bedroom suite*, I thought.

"This is Virginia and Ted Davis," Bob said. "You might remember reading about them in the paper last weekend. Their home was vandalized while they were away."

I remembered the story. Everything they owned—furniture, clothing, dishes, appliances—was stolen or broken.

"The police still have no leads," Ted Davis said. "The children lost all their toys. The insurance money will cover some of the loss, but not nearly enough. Fortunately a church down the street gave us a bed for the master bedroom." And then he paused before asking, "Is two hundred your lowest price on this suite?"

My husband was staring at me, as was the entire Davis family. Finally Bob spoke: "Honey, can we talk in the kitchen?"

I closed the door behind us. One look at my ever-generous husband told me what he was thinking. "But if we give it away, we'd be giving up the money we planned on," I reminded him.

"Debra," Bob asked, his eyes boring into me, "do we really need to make a profit off these people?"

I looked away. That money was for extras. We would still get our family vacation. But this family needed to get their lives back together. Other people at the sale were shopping for bargains; the Davises were shopping for necessities.

Back outside I told Ted Davis our price. "Free?" he exclaimed. "You mean just take it?"

"Absolutely. And you can have the stack of dishes on the table out front."

"What about the other things you need?" Bob asked. "We can put a notice in our church newsletter."

For a moment the Davises looked dumbfounded. Then Virginia Davis turned to me, "I don't know how we can thank you."

"Don't worry. Someday you'll be able to help someone else." And I thought to myself, *Someday God will give them that opportunity, just as He gave it to us.*

A few customers helped us load the bedroom suite, bedspreads and other items in the Davises' pickup truck. The two small girls were clutching pillows as they climbed into the cab, and I had the warm feeling that comes from knowing you've made a difference in someone's life.

Later that evening the phone rang, and my son told me a Mrs. Stevens was on the line, explaining, "She wondered if that bedroom suite was still for sale."

"Oh, that!" I laughed. "Tell Mrs. Stevens it's been taken." No, we didn't get $200 for that bedroom set. We got a lot more.

Debra Fulghum Bruce

• •

A man wrote a letter to the IRS: "I have been unable to sleep knowing that I have cheated on my income tax. I understated my taxable income and have enclosed a check for $150. If I still can't sleep, I will send the rest."

Brian Becker

• •

8

Let's Make a Deal!

Life—is it Door #1, Door #2, or Door #3? When it comes to financial security, it's anybody's guess. Sometimes we guess right and get the cash. Sometimes we guess wrong and get the horse laugh.

VALUE OF A DOLLAR

My children have no concept of money. In spite of our best efforts to teach them the value of the almighty dollar, they simply don't wrap their minds around the fact those little green slips of paper are actually worth something.

Oh, they like the idea of capitalism and commerce. Take them to the kids' aisle in Wal-Mart, or let them loose at Dollar General and they'll go ballistic. They've shopped alongside us for enough years to know the excitement of a sale or why buying generic is just as good as name brand or that you try to never pay full price for anything.

We're penny pinchers at heart, and if we can get something for free, or deeply discounted, all the better.

In our early married days, my husband and I struggled too hard financially to take anything for granted. Even when we're in a position to buy pricier stuff, we usually go the cheap route. We hold good stewardship as a high priority.

But my kids are another story. Years ago, we initiated the allowance thing, lining up three jars on their dressers. Save, Spend, and Church. We'd divide the money up, their eyes sparkling at the clinking of the coins. And dollar bills, whoa, that was like the lottery.

They loved the idea of saving money. It was the literal part they had trouble with. The "you have to know where the money is in order to save or spend it" theory.

We'd find dollars used as a towel for Barbie. Or quarters taking the place of checker pieces. Random pieces of money in the back seat of my car, or lying on the kitchen floor. Tucked in amidst Matchbox cars and dirty socks.

Not valued. Lost. Forgotten. We work so hard on our weekly budget, to see that even a small portion taken for granted was too much. We stopped the allowance, and haven't looked back.

Until recently. The kids and I went to lunch with my mother, otherwise known as Gee, and she offered to pay for parking. I thanked her, since I happened to be out of cash. My kids, greedy little beggars, piped up, "We're out of cash, too. We're flat broke!"

I shot them "I'll get you later" looks and smiled through my teeth.

My mother thought it was hilarious, and promptly handed them each twenty bucks. Not your best lesson in the work-equals-earn department. I guess that's a luxury of grandparenting, not worrying that every moment is a character growth opportunity.

The kids giggled and wiggled, thanked Gee profusely, and we headed on our way. Before we got home, I found my daughter's twenty rolled up in a tootsie roll shape, on top of the guest bed. My son couldn't find his bill anywhere, not sure if he'd left it in the car, in his pockets, or at Gee's house.

A thorough search resulted in nothing. Gee's solution was to slip him another twenty, so feelings would not be hurt. She's gracious that way, whereas I fall more on the "I-told-you-so" side. Then, my daughter checked the doggie bag from the schmancy restaurant (I said I was cheap), and *voila*, the case of the missing money was solved.

A friend with teenagers told me it only gets worse, that lost money is a consistent source of tension. But I'm determined. My children will know the value of a dollar if it kills me. I'm going back to the allowance, and teach my children the laws of good stewardship. Maybe I'll take a class or buy a book.

After I dig around in the sandbox for an extra buck or two.

Britta Coleman

"You have been approved for a fixed-rate mortgage. That means if interest rates go up again and you're not paying enough, we'll fix it."

••

The following sign was being carried by an employee who was on strike: "Time heals all wounds. Time and a half heals them faster!"

Earl Wilson

••

Today's Stock Market Report

Helium was up, feathers were down. Paper was stationary.

Fluorescent tubing was dimmed in light trading.

Cows steered into a bull market.

Pencils lost a few points.

Hiking equipment was trailing.

Elevators rose, while escalators continued their slow decline.

Weights were up in heavy trading.

Light switches were off.

Mining equipment hit rock bottom.

Diapers remained unchanged.

Shipping lines stayed at an even keel.

The market for raisins dried up.

Coca Cola fizzled.

Caterpillar stock inched up a bit.

Sun peaked at midday.

Balloon prices were inflated.

Scott Tissue touched a new bottom.

And batteries exploded in an attempt to recharge the market.

Chris Patterson

People always say, "He died penniless," as if it's a terrible thing. Sounds like good timing to me.

Al Cleathen

Don't bad mouth the rich—you'll never get a job from a poor person.

Kathleen Russell

HORSE POWER

One day a farmer came into the bank in Oklahoma and asked for a loan. "I want two hundred dollars."

"And what security have you?"

"I have two hundred horses," replied the farmer.

This seemed sufficient security and the loan was made.

A short while afterward the farmer came back with $2,200 in cash, paid off the note, and started to leave with the rest of the roll in his pocket.

"Why not let me take care of that money for you?" asked the banker.

Looking the banker straight in the eye, the farmer asked, "How many horses do you have?"

Tal D. Bonham

If you are stupid enough to make money your god, it'll bother you like the devil!

James E. Myers

"Ever since we were expelled from the garden I've had this worry about paying something called 'bills.'"

© Ed Sullivan

A joint checking account is never overdrawn by the wife. It is simply underdeposited by her husband.

Jim Kraus

THE USED CAR DEAL

My daughter needed a car. I hate, detest, despise, buying cars and haggling over prices. The sleazy salesmen always wear me down and talk me into buying an overpriced car regardless of whether the payments are affordable or not.

But the fact was, my daughter needed a car. I, of course, am the one with a down payment and good credit, so I had to become a part of this unsavory deal. I delayed the inevitable as long as possible with excuses, such as, "It's too cold to look for a car today," or "You can make it just one more week, can't you?"

My daughter didn't take the hint. She began to suggest places we might look. A brand new car was out of the question unless we stopped by the hospital and got a transfusion for my purse on the way. So, we "compromised." We decided to buy a former rental car, only a year old, all the extras included, and best of all NO haggling—the price is the price!

It seemed simple enough. Find a car you can afford. Buy the car. Unfortunately, the only place we could find selling previously rented cars was on the other side of the world. After driving for an hour, passing it twice unbeknown, we finally had to call for directions. Big mistake. They knew we were coming. Gerald was waiting for us outside when we arrived.

"Are you the folks that called," he asked, rubbing his hands together with drool practically foaming out of his mouth. We had to admit that we were. "Let's discuss your needs," he suggested. What he meant was, "Let's discuss your financial abilities."

He went into a prerecorded barrage about how they price their cars at giveaway prices, wholesale out the dogs, and keep only the best of the fleet for their sales lot. "We want to make your buying experience as pleasant as possible," he said, as if there was any way to sign away half your assets and have it feel pleasant.

My daughter went into the particular model and features she was looking for. I interrupted, "Something economical," I said. Gerald got my drift.

"I have several that are just what you want," he purred. "Let's go out to the lot and look around. He led us straight to a sporty little gold number. My daughter's heart jumped out of her jacket as she totally forgot about what she used to want. Dollar signs flashed in Gerald's eyes. We looked around the lot as Gerald explained the features of other cars that were available, but my daughter's eyeballs remained fixated on the gold car.

Finally, we made the enormously difficult decision of buying the first thing we saw. Back to the office we went to fill out the paper work and see how anemic my purse was going to be for the next five years or until my daughter finds a job, whichever comes first.

"I don't think I came very prepared," I said, looking at the application, which asked about home ownership, loan balances, and monthly mortgage payments. Good grief, I thought I was buying a car, not a condo. "All we need is where you work and your salary," Gerald said. "Don't worry about the rest of that stuff."

He whisked the paper out from under my pen and sped to the back room, where I presume the credit bureau was being contacted. He returned after a time with a smile like a cat that has been dating the canary. "You have great credit!" The pupils of his eyes flashed digital numbers as he calculated the commission in his head.

The payments were only about half of what I expected, but I didn't flinch a freckle. My daughter was outside in the driver's seat blowing the horn. We completed the deal without bloodshed, though it was close when he was talking me into

> The payments were only about half of what I expected, but I didn't flinch a freckle.

buying the extended warranty for a mere $20 per month extra.

Finally, we drove out of the parking lot, proud owners of a sporty, pre-owned, golden chariot, complete with full gas tank, certificate for emissions check, and promise of an extra set of keys. In the rear view mirror, I saw Gerald out on the used car lot standing by a silver car and grinning at a new customer like an alligator who has cornered a wildlife poacher.

Sheila Moss

••

Secretary (on phone): "He's gone to Washington to get a government loan to pay back what he borrowed from the bank to pay his income tax."

Tal D. Bonham

••

AN AWESOME DEAL

I was walking past Jake's Vintage Usables and Collectibles just like every day on my way home from my friend Jeremy's. Couldn't see anything to buy in the window that day; it was all the same stuff as the day before.

Mr. Jake waved as he heard the bell jingle. "Eric, my boy!" Mr. Jake is older than my grandpa and nobody knows his last name. He's practically hairless and his face is full of creases. He always looks like he's thinking of something funny. Even his ears smile at the sides of his head. "So, what's black and white and red all over?" he challenged.

"A newspaper and . . . a sunburned zebra!"

"Ha! Haven't stumped you yet."

"Anything new today?"

"Have a look." He winked and began cleaning a display case.

The shop had a good kind of moldy smell. I rummaged through bins of antique postcards and faded comic books. There was an old *Captain Zappo* that looked ok. I tucked it under my arm. Then something on the wall caught my eye. I didn't have a clock, really, just my radio alarm, but it wasn't a cat with a tail that moved back and forth like this one. The eyes swung from side to side, as if they were hunting for a mouse. I had to buy it.

I looked at the sticker on the back. It was a good deal, an awesome deal. There was enough in my wallet. Friday is allowance day, and I can do whatever I want with it. I should set aside ten percent for the collection plate, and I really am going to—it's just that there's a lot of stuff I need. Besides, my allowance is the same amount as last year. A kid my age really should get more.

> **I looked at the sticker on the back. It was a good deal, an awesome deal.**

Mr. Jake put the clock and the comic book in a bag and gave me my change. He saluted, making me smile. "Be strong and courageous, my boy!"

I slid the coins into my pocket and they jingled as I walked to the door, looking around one last time to see if there was anything else I needed. There wasn't, so on the way home I stopped at Quik-Mart and got some Mondo Bubble.

The clock fit over my dresser, right above the bike headlight I'd bought the day before, and my baseball cards. I needed a clock like that.

Before dinner, Mom took me into town with her to check out the sales. I asked her if we could buzz past Gregg's Greenlake Cycle on Woodlawn, just to look.

"Mom, stop the car!"

Right smack in the center of the window was the most awesome skateboard I had ever seen. It was a pro-board: twin-tipped, low to the ground, 42-millimeter wheels. This was no banana board.

"Will you get it for me?"

Mom rolled her eyes. "Eric, you already have a skate-board."

"But, Mom, it's three years old! It glows in the dark. The kids laugh at it. And look, it's an awesome deal."

"Good, then use your birthday money from Grandma."

"It's . . . gone. I used it for baseball cards."

She shook her head. "Well, I guess you'll just have to save up."

"Save up! How?"

"There's always the garage."

Mom had been trying to get me to clean her garage all summer. Suddenly I wanted to do it. I also did the flower beds, the fence and the windows. It would take a few weeks, but it'd be worth it.

It was hard to pass up Mr. Jake's store. After a few days, he came out and waved.

"Eric, my boy! What's black and white and red all over?"

"A newspaper and a skunk with diaper rash."

"Ha! Haven't seen much of you lately, strong and coura-geous one." He seemed older today.

"Oh, well I've been, um, busy, you know?"

Mr. Jake nodded and winked and went back into his shop. After that I took a different route home. The money in my skateboard jar was adding up.

One Friday I did stop at Mr. Jake's store. *Just to look*, I told myself. When I turned the old brass doorknob, though, it was locked. Then I saw the orange "closed" sign.

"Didn't you hear?" Jeremy called from across the street. "Mr. Jake had a heart attack. He just got home from the hospital."

I scribbled a note and slipped it through the mail slot. "A blushing panda," it said. "Be strong and courageous."

The next morning was Saturday. Before she left for work,

Mom wrapped up a casserole. "Now carry that dish carefully, Eric. Tell Mr. Jake it can be warmed up in the microwave as soon as he's ready to eat it."

When I knocked on Mr. Jake's door, he called me to come in. His voice was so thin, I barely heard him.

"Eric, my boy. Glad you could stop by!" His craggy face lit up. I'd never been in his house before. It must've been a hundred years old. The kitchen floor was covered with cracked, grey linoleum. Next to the kitchen, Mr. Jake was sitting up in bed. He seemed skinnier than usual, but maybe it was because he was still in his pajamas. I showed him the casserole, and his eyes seemed to mist up a little.

"Thank you, Eric. Thank your mother for me. She's a good woman."

The refrigerator was one of those short, white ones with the rounded corners and "Frigidaire" written across the front in chrome. I opened the door to put the casserole in. All that was inside was a carton of orange juice and some fuzzy bread. That was it. Mr. Jake wasn't watching. I didn't want to be nosy, but I opened his cupboard doors one by one. In the first cupboard were a few mismatched dishes, pots and pans, and cups in all sizes. In the next were a cake mix, a can of sardines and some oatmeal. The rest of the cupboards were empty.

We played checkers while he drank a glass of orange juice. He offered some to me, but I said, "No thank you." When he said good-bye, his voice didn't sound quite as thin.

At home I emptied the money out of my skateboard jar and counted it just like I did every day. There was a little more than enough and today was the day. I thought about those narrow wheels and the feel of the rough pavement under them. My mind invented new jumps and turns. The money filled my two hands, and coins slipped out between my fingers. I made it into a little pile.

There was this funny feeling in my chest, though. I remembered the cake mix and the sardines. I took ten percent of the money out of the pile and set it aside for Sunday. There must be a lot of Mr. Jakes.

There was just enough left. I put it in my wallet and threw on my jacket. I was going to ride the board back so Jeremy could see it.

I walked past Mr. Jake's store. A few blocks ahead were the painted bicycles on the wall of Gregg's Greenlake Cycle. The wallet bulged in my back pocket.

At the corner I had to wait for the light. Roasting turkey smells came from the supermarket deli. I wondered if Mr. Jake had eaten Mom's casserole yet. The sign flashed red at me, "Joe's Super Foods."

The light changed. I only had ten seconds to cross this street. The cars waited at the crosswalk as my light turned yellow, then red. I turned away from the curb and walked into Joe's.

I filled the cart with pears, baked beans, cans of tuna, milk, and bread. I even bought a chicken. Maybe I could help him cook it.

The clerk rang up the sale and I slid my money across the counter. It was a good deal; an awesome deal.

Katherine Grace Bond

••

A money-grabber is anyone who grabs more money than you can.

Bob Phillips

••

CRACKED UP

I was helping a friend of mine with his roadside farm stand when a man stopped by and asked how much the eggs were.

"Sixty cents for the small, 70 cents for the medium, 90 cents for the large, and 30 cents for the cracked ones," I answered.

"All right," he said.

"Crack me a dozen of the large ones."

Russell Long

MARGARET AND HER PENNIES

E very Monday morning, my friend Jim and I eat breakfast at Bob Evans and swap war stories. Jim pastors an inner-city church, and his stories have more meat and gristle than mine.

One morning he told me about Margaret. Margaret is an eighty-year-old widow in his church. She lives in a retirement center and ventures out once a week to buy groceries at Safeway. Margaret, Jim reports, is a sweet lady, though that hasn't always been the case. She told Jim that when she was younger she was not a good person, but God has slowly changed her. Occasionally, God builds the house overnight, but most times God nails up one board each day. Margaret was a board each day.

Several years ago, Margaret felt God wanted her to do something for her inner-city church. So she prayed about it, and after a while the Lord told her to save all her pennies for the children of the church. Margaret was hoping for something a little grander, but didn't complain. A person has to start somewhere, she told Jim. So every year at Christmas, she wrapped up her pennies, about ten dollars' worth, and gave them to her church. she told them it was for the kids and not to spend it on pew cushions.

One afternoon a lady down the hall from Margaret came

to visit. She noticed Margaret's mayonnaise jar full of pennies. She asked her why she was saving pennies. Margaret told her it was for the kids at church.

"I don't have a church," the lady said. "Can I save up my pennies and give them to the kids in your church?"

"Suit yourself," Margaret said.

Before long, thirty folks in the retirement center were saving their pennies for the kids.

Every Wednesday, they climb on the retirement center's bus and drive to the Safeway. They steer their carts up and down the aisles, then stand in line at the checkout counter. They put their groceries on the moving belt and watch as each price pops up on the display. When the checker calls the total, the old folks count out the money a bill at a time. Then they ask for the change in pennies. They count that out, too, one penny at a time. The other customers stand behind them and roll their eyes. They don't know a work of God is underway.

The next year at Christmastime, the women loaded up their jars and took their pennies, twenty thousand of them, to the church Christmas party. The kids staggered from the Christmas party, their pockets bursting with pennies.

When the kids found out who was behind the pennies, they wanted to visit the retirement center and sing Christmas carols. Pastor Jim took them in Big Blue, the church bus. They assembled in the dining room. Jim watched from the back row. In front of him sat one of the retirement center ladies. Jim didn't know her, had never seen her. She was explaining to a visitor what was going on.

"These children, you see, they're from our church, and they've come to visit us. We're awfully close."

The next week, one of the men in the retirement center passed away. Jim came and conducted the memorial service right there at the retirement center, which is fast becoming the new church annex.

All of this, mind you, began with Margaret in her apartment praying to the Lord to let her do a mighty work. She admits now that she was a little disappointed when God told her to save her pennies. She was hoping for a more flamboyant ministry. She didn't want to start with pennies. Then she thought back on her own life and how sometimes God builds houses one board each day.

Phillip Gulley

Really Charles! A Clergy Discount?!

....

The buck stops here!

A sign on the desk of President Harry S. Truman

....

Acknowledgments

Alley, Ken. *The Big Book of Church Humor.* York, NE: iUniverse, Inc, 2003. Used by permission.

Bigger, Margaret G. Charlotte, NC: A. Borough Books, 1999.

Bolton, Martha. *If the Pasta Wiggles.* Ventura, CA: Vine Books, 1996. Used by permission of author.

———. *Didn't My Skin Used to Fit?* Grand Rapids, MI: Bethany, a division of Baker Books, 2000.

———. *Cooking with Hot Flashes.* Grand Rapids, MI: Bethany, a division of Baker Books, 2004.

Bordon, David and Tom Winters. *God's Roadmap for Moms.* New York: Time Warner, 2005.

Bonham, Tal D. *The Treasury of Clean Jokes.* Nashville, TN: Broadman & Holman, 1997.

Browne, Jill Conner. *Sweet Potato Queens Cookbook.* New York: Three Rivers Press, a division of Random House, 2003.

Cohl, Aaron. *The Friar's Club Encyclopedia of Jokes.* New York: Black Dog & Leventhal, 1997.

Coleman, Britta. "Value of a Dollar." Used by permission. Britta Coleman (www.brittacoleman.com) is an award-winning author, journalist, and inspirational speaker. Her debut novel, *Potter Springs*, won the Lone Star Scribe Award, and her "Practically Parenting" column is published as a regular newspaper feature. Britta lives in Fort Worth, TX with her husband, two children, and two Chihuahuas.

Fadiman, Charles. *American Treasury.* New York: Harper, 1955.

Fann, Joey. *The Way Back to Mayberry.* Nashville: Broadman & Holman, © 2001 by Joey Fann. Reprinted and Used by permission.

Farmer, Debbie. "Garage Saling." Debbie Farmer writes the syndicated column "Family Daze". Her essays have been published in *Family Circle*, *Readers Digest*, *Family Fun*, over 150 regional parenting magazines and more. For information on running her column in your publication or to receive the free Family Daze monthly e-column, visit her website: www.familydaze.com

Fowler, Gene. *Beau James.* New York: A.M. Kelley, 1973.

Gulley, Phillip. *Hometown Tales.* New York: Harper, ©1998 by Phillip Gulley. Used by permission.

Harvey, Paul Jr. *For What It's Worth.* New York: Bantam, 1992.

Higney, Gene Michael. *Life as an IRS Agent.* ©2006 by Gene Michael Higney.

Taken from *1001 Humorous Illustrations for Public Speaking* by Michael Hodgin. Copyright ©1994 by Michael Hodgin. Used by permission of The Zondervan Corporation.

Hollingsworth, Mary. Administered by Shady Oaks Studio, 1507 Shirley Way, Bedford, TX 76022. Used by permission.

Kane, Madeleine Begun. "Dear Cardholder." Copyright MadeleineBegunKane@Madkane.com. Madeleine Begun

Kane is a humorist, song parodist, and public speaker based in New York City. Her website is http://www.madkane.com. All rights reserved.

———. "If It's Broken, Don't Fix It." Copyright © MadeleineBegunKane@Madkane.com. Madeleine Begun Kane is a humorist, song parodist, and public speaker based in New York City. Her website is http://www.madkane.com. All rights reserved.

Kennedy, Pamela. "Fund Raising Follies." © 1997 Pamela Kennedy. Used by permission. Pamela Kennedy is a freelance writer of short stories, articles, essays, and children's books. She draws her material from her own experiences and memories, adding highlights from her imagination to enhance the story. Pamela currently resides in Honolulu, Hawaii, with her family.

———. "Adventures in Realtyland." © 1999 Pamela Kennedy. Used by permission. Pamela Kennedy is a freelance writer of short stories, articles, essays, and children's books. She draws her material from her own experiences and memories, adding highlights from her imagination to enhance the story. Pamela currently resides in Honolulu, Hawaii, with her family.

Kraus, James. *Bloopers, Blunders, Quips, Jokes, and Quotes.* Wheaton, IL: Tyndale, 2005. Used by permission.

Lyles, Cleon. *Wish I'd Said That.* Morrilton, AR: ©1970 by Cleon Lyles.

Mahoney, Kathryn. *Cracked at Birth: One Madcap Mom's Thoughts on Motherhood, Marriage & Burnt Meatloaf.* Deadwood, OR: Wyatt-MacKenzie Publishing, Inc., 2005. www.crackedatbirth.com. www.wymacpublishing.com.

Meurer, Dave. *Stark Raving Dad.* ©2002 by Dave Meurer. Used by permission. Dave Meurer is the author of *Mistake It Like a Man: An Imperfect Guide to Romance, Kids, and Secret Service Motorcades.*

———. *Boyhood Daze.* Grand Rapids: Fleming H. Revell, a division of Baker, 1999.

Moss, Sheila. "The Used Car Deal." Used by permission. Sheila Moss is a self-syndicated humor columnist from Tennessee. She is best known as an Internet columnist, but also has been published in book anthologies, magazines, and newspapers. www.humorcolumnist.com

———. "Dear IRS." Used by permission. Sheila Moss is a self-syndicated humor columnist from Tennessee. She is best known as an Internet columnist, but also has been published in book anthologies, magazines, and newspapers. www.humorcolumnist.com.

Myers, James. *A Treasury of Religious Humor.* South Bend, IN: And Books, 1993. Used by permission.

Offutt, James. Used by permission. www.jasonoffutt.com.

Phillips, Bob. *Great Thoughts and Funny Sayings.* Wheaton, IL: Tyndale, 1993.

Phillips, Cathy Lee. *Gutsy Little Flower.* Canton, GA: Patchwork Press, 2001. Used by permission. www.cathyleephillips.com.

Prairie Home Companion. *Pretty Good Joke Book.* Minneapolis, MN: Highbridge Company, 2003.

Reid, Don. *Sunday Morning Memories.* Green Forest, AR: New Leaf Press, 2004. Used by permission.

Renfroe, Anita. *The Purse Driven Life.* Colorado Springs: Navpress, 2005 by Anita Renfroe. Used by permission of NavPress, Colorado Springs, CO. All rights reserved.

Russell, Kathleen. *Money...Now You Have It. Now You Don't.* Seattle: Walrus Productions, 1994. Used by permission. www.walrusproductions.com.

Snyder, James L. "*As the Old Year Fades, So Does My Memory.*" Used by permission. The Rev. James L. Snyder is pastor of the Family of God Fellowship. www.whatafellowship.com. He is also an award winning author and columnist. Contact him at jamessnyder2@att.net.

Schmeidler, Elizabeth. "Never Underestimate the Power of a

Penny." Used by permission. Elizabeth Schmeidler is happily married and mother to three wonderful sons. Also a singer/songwriter, Elizabeth has recorded three CD's of inspirational music, most of which she composed herself. Her music can be heard at www.sacredheartradio.net. As an author of novels, short stories, children's stories, and poetry, she continues to write and sing in her pursuit to do God's will. She can be contacted through the above website or at cdmusic@eaglecom.net.

————. "Inflation and the Tooth Fairy." Used by permission. Elizabeth Schmeidler is happily married and mother to three wonderful sons.   Also a singer/songwriter, Elizabeth has recorded three CD's of inspirational music, most of which she composed herself. Her music can be heard at www.sacredheartradio.net.   As an author of novels, short stories, children's stories, and poetry, she continues to write and sing in her pursuit to do God's will. She can be contacted through the above website or at cdmusic@eaglecom.net.

St. John-Gilbert, Rachel. *Wake Up Laughing* published by Barbour Publishing, Inc. Uhrichsville, OH: Barbour, 1985. Used by permission.

Torrey, Isabel Wolseley. "Dogs, People Much Alike." Used by permission.

————. "Why Not Pet Exemptions?" Used by permission.

Vredevelt, Pam. *Espresso For a Woman's Spirit*. Sisters, OR: Multnomah, 2000.

Wall, P. S. *My Love is Free...But the Rest of Me Don't Come Cheap.* Nashville: Rutledge Hill, 1997. Used by permission of author. Paula Wall is the author of the national bestselling novel, *The Rock Orchard*. Her upcoming novel, *The Wilde Women* (Atria) will be available in April 2007.

————. *If I Were A Man, I'd Marry Me.* New York: Ballantine, 1999. Used by permission of author. Paula Wall is the author of the national bestselling novel, *The Rock*

Orchard. Her upcoming novel, *The Wilde Women* (Atria) will be available in April 2007.

Walker, Laura Jensen. *Through the Rocky Road and into the Rainbow Sherbet.* Grand Rapids, MI: Fleming Revell, a division of Baker Book House, 2002.

Will-Harris, Daniel. "Why I Shop On-line." Used by permission. Daniel Will-Harris is a writer, graphic designer and bon vivant who believes in the power of love and chocolate. His humorous email www.SchmoozeLetter.com goes to over 30,000 happy subscribers (sign up and be number 30,001!). The stories have been collected into his latest book, *"My Wife & Times,"* which said wife personally handed to the British royals. MoMA in New York called his design work "truly unique." His graphic design, wrist watch design, and other work can be seen at www.Will-Harris.com

Wright, Rusty and Linda Raney. *500 Clean Jokes and Humorous Stories.* Uhrichsville, OH: Barbour, 1985. Used by permission.

Youngman, Henny. *The Best Little Book of One Liners.* Philadelphia: Running Press, 1992.

A Note from
the Editors

This original book was created by the Books and Inspirational Media Division of Guideposts, the world's leading inspirational publisher. Founded in 1945 by Dr. Norman Vincent Peale and his wife Ruth Stafford Peale, Guideposts helps people from all walks of life achieve their maximum personal and spiritual potential. Guideposts is committed to communicating positive, faith-filled principles for people everywhere to use in successful daily living.

Other publications include award-winning magazines like *Guideposts, Angels on Earth, Sweet 16,* and *Positive Thinking,* best-selling books, and outreach services that demonstrate what can happen when faith and positive thinking are applied to day-to-day life.

For more information, visit us online at www.guideposts.org, call (800) 431-2344, or write Guideposts, 39 Seminary Hill Road, Carmel, New York 10512.